The Rules of Poker

The
Rules
of
Poker

ESSENTIALS FOR EVERY GAME

Lou Krieger and
Sheree Bykofsky

LYLE STUART
Kensington Publishing Corp.
www.kensingtonbooks.com

LYLE STUART BOOKS are published by

Kensington Publishing Corp.
850 Third Avenue
New York, NY 10022

All Kensington titles, imprints, and distributed lines are available at special quantity discounts for bulk purchases for sales promotions, premiums, fund-raising, educational, or institutional use. Special book excerpts or customized printings can also be created to fit specific needs. For details, write or phone the office of the Kensington special sales manager: Kensington Publishing Corp., 850 Third Avenue, New York, NY 10022, attn: Special Sales Department; phone 1-800-221-2647.

Lyle Stuart is a trademark of Kensington Publishing Corp.

First printing: December 2006

10 9 8 7 6 5 4 3 2 1

Printed in the United States of America

ISBN 0-8184-0660-7

CONTENTS

Part One: Reponsibilities and Etiquette

♥ Chapter 1 The House—General Rights and Procedures

◆ Chapter 3 **Player Conduct, Etiquette, and Integrity**

Part Two: Structures of Play

♣ Chapter 4 **The Deck and Cards**

♥ Chapter 5 **Betting Structures**

CONTENTS

Part Three: Rules of the Games

♠ **Chapter 6 Texas Hold'em, Omaha, and Other Community-Card (Board) Games**

♠ **Chapter 7 Stud Games**

Part Four: Tournaments

♥ Chapter 9 Tournament Rules

CONTENTS

Part Five: Rules We'd Like to Change

INTRODUCTION

Arguments break out by the minute in card rooms across the country. They happen all the time. Scores of rules exist concerning fairness and etiquette in poker, but they're not uniform, instead varying from place to place. Many rules are generally accepted, but sometimes card room managers, floor supervisors, and tournament directors just don't know them all, fail to make their policies known, or interpret rules to the letter of the law when decisions should be made in the interests of fairness and in keeping with the traditions and best interests of the game.

WHY THIS BOOK IS NEEDED

Rules differ between tournaments and cash games, even in the same card room or casino. And sometimes a rule will change depending on which floor supervisor is called upon to make a ruling. Things are even worse in home games; typically, tempers flare and cards go flying. This book offers a solution.

The Rules of Poker lays out all of the best poker rules as comprehensively as possible. Whenever possible we provide varying rules, with the preferred rule first. The index is comprehensive, easy to use, and thorough.

But our intention is to provide much more than just a dry rule book. Dry rule books won't hold anyone's interest, and we certainly don't want that. Besides the rules themselves, we've filled this book with boxed sidebars of anecdotes from dealers, players, and poker-room staff about why disputes have broken out and how they were settled. We're hoping that you, the reader, will actually hear the gunshots.

Other games and sports have official rules of etiquette, but until today, no such single book has been accepted in the world of poker. Before the *Official Scrabble ® Player's Dictionary* was released, people divorced over whether or not "belting" could take an "s." Through interviews, research, and personal experience, with a dash of fun and the voices of many authorities—particularly the Tournament Directors Association (TDA)—we offer the world of poker THE book that will settle poker arguments and allow players to concentrate on the business at hand—scooping in large sums of money.

If you're a floor supervisor, dealer, or involved in the management of a room, this book provides a logical basis for the interpretation and implementation of rules consistent with those found in most poker establishments. If you are a player, knowing the rules provides information you can use when you're involved in a dispute at the poker table. It also puts you in the know about how games are started, run, managed, and broken down, as well as procedures followed by dealers, floor supervisors, tournament directors, poker managers, and others involved in the effective management of an efficient card room or casino.

If you're a home-game player, and particularly if you

host a home game, these rules can prove valuable to you in structuring your game so that it resembles a casino game as closely as possible. While home games generally include variations of poker that are never found in casinos or card rooms (and even include games that are made up on the spot), the rules will provide guidelines with which you can manage and govern your games. After all, the best way to stop a dispute is to prevent it from starting in the first place.

Poker's growing popularity has paralleled that of personal computers. If you're a player who has learned poker online and is now contemplating play in a casino, these rules will teach you many of the differences between online play and poker in a "brick and mortar" casino. For example, it's a breech of poker etiquette to act out of turn by folding, calling, betting, or raising before the action gets around to you. But in a casino, the only governor on your behavior is you, along with any comments that might come your way from the dealer or supervisors if you persist in acting in a fashion that's at odds with poker's rules, tradition, and etiquette.

This book covers poker as played online as well as in traditional casinos. Some of the things that can be done—although they really shouldn't—such as acting out of turn, are impossible online, because the online poker site's software precludes that sort of thing from happening.

OUR BOOK'S OBJECTIVE

The underlying objective of this book is to provide a comprehensive set of rules along with anecdotal information that will enable you, the reader, to gain a perspective of what's fair, what's in keeping with the traditions and history of poker, what's best for the situation at hand, and what makes for honest and equitable procedures in managing and playing the game.

As poker players, our philosophy was to provide sufficiently detailed rules so as to allow a poker supervisor to understand which rule would apply in any given situation, to provide the decision maker with the power to rule in the best interest of the game, and to explain his ruling clearly and simply to the affected parties so that it will be accepted as fair and just by all concerned. A related objective is to bring more unity to poker, so that rules become standardized as much as possible from one locale to the next. We believe this will go a long way to promulgating poker as the world's card game of choice.

Our goal is to provide sufficient anecdotal material to clarify situations and spread light into many of those fuzzy, dark corners of poker play, as well as to provide a good read to anyone interested in *The Rules of Poker*. That's one reason you'll find Interpretation Notes scattered throughout the book. Sometimes a rule all by itself is not sufficient to provide the framework required to make it well understood and easy to apply. These notes are meant to be contextual—examples and "for instances" are included—so that anyone reading the rule will have a perspective for understanding and applying the rule.

WHAT WE ASSUME ABOUT YOU

This is not a poker instructional book, and we assume you are not picking this up to learn the basics of play. It's not

. . . .

INTRODUCTION

designed to teach you which starting hands to play and which to avoid, and it won't explain tactical and strategic ploys that will increase your playing skill in any of a variety of poker games.

Rather, we assume you know how to play, have been playing for a while, and have an interest in learning and promulgating a recommended set of poker rules.

Even if you're a real poker maven—an expert who has been interpreting poker rules in your casino or card room— you'll still benefit from what we have to offer. Some of our suggested rules will go a long way to help unify poker and bring some much needed consistency to what has become a global game. You'll also have a chance to see how a variety of poker supervisors have dealt with rule interpretations, which may reinforce what you already know. You may even encounter some situations you've never thought of before now.

HOW TO USE THIS BOOK

This is primarily a reference book, although we hope it serves as a tutorial for anyone who is concerned with the proper play of poker. We envision our potential readers as players, supervisors, dealers, and those producing poker content for television and other media.

There's no need to read it from cover to cover to understand where we're coming from. You can begin where you'd like to, and dive into this book on a game-by-game basis if that's your desire. But we do recommend reading the beginning chapters first. They deal with rules and etiquette that pertain to all games, and this material will provide you with a feel for poker's unique environment and help you to make interpretations of situations you encounter that are not explicitly covered by the rules.

HOW THIS BOOK IS ORGANIZED

We've organized this book in layers from the top down, starting with global aspects such as poker's Prime Directive and the overall management of the game, and finishing with the nuts and bolts of many of the games you'll play. We've also included two topics of special interest. Not only does the book's format allow easy access to the rules that govern a given situation, it packages these rules into related groups, ensuring that each chapter's theme—and its corresponding discussion—is self-contained.

Following our introduction, chapter 1 covers the global structure and overall management of the game. There are certain truisms that are applicable to all forms of poker, in all venues, and you'll find the rules that govern them ordered and detailed here. From poker's Prime Directive to the policing of conduct to the general running of the games, this section creates the framework within which the game is played. The Prime Directive—actually *two* directives— govern all other aspects of poker play:

- ✓ One player per hand
- ✓ Cards speak

Any floor supervisor, poker manager, or even a player who runs a home game can take a giant step toward elimi- nating dissent, arguments, and irritated players by making decisions predicated on these two overriding, universal con- cepts. The game of poker is filled with tradition, and we believe those traditions should be honored to the greatest extent possible. This chapter discusses their importance in making decisions and rules that reflect poker's historical antecedents and serve as guidance for making decisions that are in the best interests of the game.

Chapter 2 looks at more specific concepts and rules governing the running of rooms and tables. In all instances, our perspective remains the same: fairness. Some of these rules are hard and fast, whereas others have local variations or are otherwise open to some interpretation. Therefore, when a narrowly interpreted rule flies in the face of fairness, equitable decision making, or poker's traditions, we strongly urge that the spirit of the rule—rather than the letter of the law—be followed. Included here are the play-specific policies and procedures that are nonetheless applicable to all poker games, and cover such things as cash on the table, table stakes, "playing behind," and the number of bets and raises permitted in games.

Chapter 3 switches the focus from the management of the game to the players and their actions. Players are as bound by tradition and etiquette as management, and knowing what constitutes proper conduct is a key element in preventing rules, ethics, or etiquette violations. *Etiquette* can be defined as an unwritten code that governs behavior, but we've done some of the writing of that "unwritten" code for you here. These rules are as much a part of poker as the cards and chips themselves. And while violating some of the rules may be merely a social faux pas or minor gaffe, other breaches of etiquette are enough to get you tossed from the game.

The second part of the book moves from the actions of game management and the players to the mechanics and trappings of play itself. Chapter 4 is a procedural chapter detailing deck composition, the rankings of hands, the number of betting rounds, what comprises a mixed deal, and even mechanical shuffling machines. We also include here miscellaneous procedural topics such as button types and placement, seat- and table-change rules, third-man-walking rules, and the establishment and administration of *must-move* games.

Chapter 5, by comparison, focuses on the various betting structures and the handling of the pot(s). Included here are rules governing fixed-limit poker, pot-limit, and no-limit, as well as less common structures such as spread limits and "playing overs." We also include here a series of rules on kill pots and showdowns. Kill pots, found in many casinos, occur after a triggering event—one player winning two pots in a row, or scooping both sides of the pot in a high-low split game—and cause the stakes to double on the next hand. We've covered all the common kill pot situations and procedures you're likely to encounter. And in the rules governing showdowns, you'll learn the proper way of handling tied pots, side pots, and disbursing odd chips.

The third part of the book begins our look at the rules of specific poker games. Chapter 6 examines "board" games, including Texas hold'em, Omaha, Omaha/8, pineapple, crazy pineapple, and Tahoe. Chapter 7 details the "stud" games such as five-card stud, six-card stud, seven-card stud, seven-stud/8, razz, and Mississippi seven-card stud. Chapter 8 moves on to the "draw" games such as draw-with-joker, California lowball, jacks back, Kansas City lowball, and the deuce-to-seven and ace-to-five versions of triple-draw lowball. Other, miscellaneous games, are included here as well.

Chapter 9 is all about tournaments. Literally. Tournaments are so distinctive and important to today's poker world that they require a specific chapter donated entirely to the topic. Tournament poker is very different from cash games, and these rules are offered with a debt of gratitude to the Tournament Directors Association, a voluntary group of poker industry professionals who are working to unify tournament rules worldwide. Founded by Linda Johnson, Jan Fisher, Matt Savage, and Dave Lamb, the TDA includes floor supervisors, tournament directors, poker managers, poker theorists, and others whose hard efforts continue toward the goal of a viable and unified set of procedures for tournament poker, and we thank them for their efforts.

And finally, chapter 10 (Rules We'd Like to Change) gave us a chance to get a few things off our chests. You can't write a book like this without encountering a few rules and procedures you'd like to see replaced, scrapped, or modified. You may agree or disagree with us at one point or another; we realize that someone had reason for establishing these rules in the first place. But whichever side of the fence you're on, we hope this serves as food for thought and discussion.

There you have it. An index is not something most casual readers get excited about. But for this book, we devoted a substantial amount of attention to it. The effective index in this book allows anyone to quickly dial into areas of concern wherein they may be called to arbitrate a dispute, disagreement, or misunderstanding. If we've done our job properly, any supervisor will be able to find the appropriate section of the book in order to rule on a dispute, even when acting in the heat of battle.

Regardless of whether he or she is asked to rule on

whether or not a hand is a "dead hand," whether or not a raise in a no-limit game is the minimum required amount, whether a misdeal took place and the cards will have to be returned to the dealer to be dealt again, which player must show down his hand first at the conclusion of play, or any of the other numerous issues that arise in poker games, this book's index is easily addressable by topic and subject and will make it easy for decision making.

WILL THIS BOOK PREVENT ALL FUTURE ARGUMENTS AT THE POKER TABLE?

Even though we consider this book to be the ultimate argument settler, we'd be naïve if we thought that this little book would not only resolve but prevent all arguments at the poker table. If we made that claim, you'd be foolish to believe us. Debates and disputes can't be prevented at the poker table any more than a civil code prevents one person from suing another in the world at large. But disputes can be diffused and resolved, and for anyone who is in control of his or her emotions at the poker table, the rules, procedures, and adherence to the traditions and etiquette of poker that we've presented will help continue to tame and civilize the poker environment. And what's poker without a little passion and adrenaline, anyway?

Although rules still vary from one card room to another, progress has been made in recent years toward the unification of poker rules. Things are a lot better now than they were in the Wild West. In those days, men like Wild Bill Hickok, Doc Holliday, and scores of others weren't afraid to enforce the rules of poker *their* way, and if you were on the wrong end of one of their decisions it could bring your poker career to a sudden and permanent stop. Aces and eights is said to be the hand that Wild Bill "went out" with, and it's now famously known as "the dead man's hand."

We hope this book will represent a giant step forward in the unification of poker rules from place to place, while giving you, the reader, an understanding—from rules, examples, and vignettes provided by tournament directors and poker floor supervisors—of the rules and etiquette surrounding poker.

But poker has come of age in recent years. With poker discussion groups on the Internet, and television carrying poker programming all hours of the day and night, great steps forward have been made in the unification of poker rules and etiquette. There are still significant differences in rules from one location to another, however, as well as major differences between the rules of play and procedures found in casinos and those found in home games, country clubs, fraternity houses, and other locales where private games are run more informally, and sometimes by different rules altogether.

ACKNOWLEDGMENTS

Thank you to the following people for providing anecdotes and rules: Foremost, we are indebted to the Tournament Directors Association (TDA) founders Linda Johnson, Jan Fisher, Matt Savage, and Dave Lamb, who have provided us with the TDA rules, which are designated herein with an asterisk. We also wish to thank them for anecdotes taken from a lifetime of tournament direction, and for their willingness to listen to our questions and suggest commonsense solutions to what otherwise might have remained vexing poker quandaries. The authors are also grateful to Donna Marks, Mike Cappelletti, Matt Lessinger, and everyone who contributed rules and anecdotes. The authors have edited and paraphrased some of the anecdotes presented herein with the kind permission of the contributors.

Thanks, too, for editorial assistance and suggestions provided by Deirdre Quinn, Mike O'Malley, and Haley Hintze. Others who have helped the authors immeasurably include Paul Avrin, Nolan Dalla, Alan Schoonmaker, David Apostolico, Gary Carson, and Tom Gitto, along with Caroline Woods, Janet Rosen, Michael Cooper, Carolyn George, Michael Jacobson, J. Phillip Vogel, Alison Kullman Don Pettifer, Levi Rothman, Rita Rosenkranz, Katharine Sands, Rob Miller, Ashley Adams, Melanie Reid, Ephraim Rosenbaum, Kathleen Dumas, Jan Dixon, Terrence, Vince, and every poker player we have ever met, befriended, or argued with.

Also, warm thanks to our editor, Richard Ember, as well as to Michaela Hamilton, Arthur Maisel, Elleanore Waka, Maureen Cuddy, and everyone else at Kensington who helped with our books.

♥ ♠ ♦ ♣

PART ONE

Responsibilities
and
Etiquette

♦ ♣ ♥ ♠

CHAPTER 1

THE HOUSE—GENERAL RIGHTS AND PROCEDURES

1.1 THE PRIME DIRECTIVE

Fans of *Star Trek* know all about the Prime Directive. It overrode all other considerations and was based on the right of each sentient species to live in accordance with its normal cultural evolution. The Prime Directive took precedence over any and all other considerations, and carried with it the highest moral obligation.

Well, you don't have to leap four centuries into the future to find a prime directive in operation. All you need do is sit down at a poker game. Poker, like *Star Trek,* has a few rules that override and supersede all others. In fact, many of the rules that you'll find in existence during a poker game were drawn out of these two rules.

We've never heard them referred to as poker's prime directives before, but like many of our readers we've all been weaned on *Star Trek,* and the idea of an overriding, overarching directive makes perfect sense to us.

Poker has two prime directives. Each equally important, and without either, there could be no game. With both directives in play, and competitors who adhere to the spirit of these two directives as well as to the letter of the law, a game can run smoothly.

The two directives are very simple and easily understood, though each provides substantial food for thought. The more you think about these two directives, the more you'll see in them. We'll return to these directives throughout the book, but we'll introduce them here in their most basic, elemental, simple form. Poker's prime directives are:

- ✓ One player per hand
- ✓ Cards speak

Let's look at each directive in a bit more detail, which will help put them into some perspective for you as well as assist in seeing how they apply to so many facets of poker.

1.2 ONE PLAYER PER HAND

Poker is not a team competition, and each player is responsible for playing his or her hand without advice or assistance, either directly given or provided inadvertently by other players, dealers, or spectators to the game. It is the responsibility of all players in a game to make sure that this overriding directive is held firm.

The ramifications are broader than you might imagine. Not only does this mean that you cannot ask your neighbor, who may or may not be involved in the hand, what you should do or how you might play your hand—that goes without saying—but your neighbor also bears a responsibility not to assist you.

If you folded your hand while others are still contesting a pot, it is a serious breach of ethics to mention the cards that you folded, or even to groan or curse if a card that could have helped you hits the board. It provides information that may help or hinder the hand's remaining players.

It is also the reason why it's so critically important for players to act in turn. If you toss your hand into the muck before it is your turn to act, you have given some potentially significant information to all the players who act after you do in the betting order. Perhaps the fact that you folded out of turn will provide the wherewithal for an opponent to raise, because now he is the last person to act and believes he may well be able to steal the pot. If you had not acted, he might merely have called—or even folded his hand— because he would have less information about your intentions before he acted. Since you might have had a powerhouse hand instead of a weak one, that possibility alone might have caused your opponent to believe he had a much smaller chance to bluff successfully, and he may have folded, thereby changing dramatically the outcome of that hand.

If you look at the flop in a Texas hold'em game and see two hearts on board, you are violating the one player per hand rule if you were to mention to another player that you folded a hand with two hearts in it. If you're overheard, one of your opponents—who might also have two hearts in his hand and is trying to determine whether to continue on in the pot with his flush draw—will now have additional information regarding the chances of completing his hand. It's one thing to draw for a flush when nine unseen cards of your suit are theoretically available to you. It's quite another thing entirely to learn that your chances have been significantly reduced because you know that your opponent has folded two of those nine hearts that were otherwise unaccounted for.

A spectator, or another player, who looks at someone's hand and mutters, "Whoa, buddy; you've got a straight draw," is clearly violating the one player per hand rule. So is a dealer who makes comments regarding the nature of the cards in sight, or gives advice to a player on how to play his hand.

As you examine the more detailed rules, you may realize that all of the rules and punishments for cheating at poker are, in fact, violations of the one player per hand rule. Collusion by two players, marked cards, signals, cold decks— you know, you've seen all the movies—are methods cheaters design to circumvent that basic directive.

It's one player per hand, first, last, and always. No hints, no comments, no statements, however innocently or altruistically rendered, that might lift the fog from one player's eyes and provide information to him that he did not infer or deduce for himself.

The following tale was submitted by poker author Mike Cappelletti.

TOPIC

Inducing Action: The Case of the Bounty Hunter

Mike participated in the first Poker Author Challenge at the Trump Taj Mahal in Atlantic City, organized by Sheree Bykofsky and sponsored by *Poker Life* magazine.

Fifteen poker authors attended, including Mike and Sheree and Lou. The authors were bounties in that anyone who knocked one out would win two autographed poker books from the Borders book table.

Mike enjoyed the event and deemed it a success, but one episode annoyed him, which Mike hopes "might point toward some future corrective poker legislation. Compared to many established sports, poker tournaments are still in the early stages and many problems and complicated situations will occur where equity should be restored."

In Mike's words, as he reported in *Cardplayer* magazine:

Late in the tournament, down to fewer than three tables, where two tables (eighteen players) would get into the money, on my little blind, I picked up a four-deuce suited. Each of eight players had anted 200 and the blinds were 2,000–4,000. I had dwindled down to about 25,000 in chips, and it was folded around to me. The big blind in back of me had about 30,000 in chips and was a rather solid player. What would you do here?

Simply put, I really wanted the 7,600 chips already in the pot—so I went all-in on my four-deuce. It was unlikely that the big blind would have a great hand and in this "near-the-bubble" situation, he would be reluctant to put in most of his chips on a medium hand.

Note that even if he did call with two big overcards, I would merely be about a 3–2 underdog. But if he called with a big pocket pair, I would only win about one time in five. All in all, this speculation has a relatively high probability of success especially when compared with the odds of winning most no-limit hold'em confrontations.

The big blind started thinking and counted his chips. It looked like he wanted to fold. After he had thought for several seconds, one of the other uninvolved players said, "He's a bounty. Knock him out and you get two free books." Then another player said, "He bluffs a lot." Needless to say, I did not appreciate these comments.

Fortunately for me, he chose to fold, so I did manage to steal the blind/antes. But what if that gratuitous advice had talked him into calling? All casinos have rules against giving advice during play. Would I have had any recourse against the two "illegal" advisers? Under the current rules, probably not.

Since a casino can invoke disciplinary penalties, the two illegal advisers could have been penalized with disqualification (unlikely) or penalty box minutes or even a fine. But is a tournament director authorized to adjust chip holdings in order to restore equity?

Suppose the big blind had made some motion that looked like he was starting to fold his ace-nine. Then he apparently listened to the two advisers, decided to call, and I lost. What would be the best ruling? This will happen again. If poker is to be accepted as a serious (eventually Olympic) sport, we will need good rules to handle these situations."

Sheree Responds

Sheree disagrees with the people who run the poker room at the Taj who feel that players are told in advance that there is a bounty and there's no harm done when a player mentions a known fact at a table. Sheree feels that the best rule is one that mimics what is compulsory online, namely, that when a player is all-in, all "chatting" at the table shall cease, in particular any chatting about the game or hand. If a rule such as this is violated, a penalty shall be invoked. But Sheree disagrees with Mike's suggestion that chips be reallocated after they are distributed. Other penalties, such as a ten-minute time-out, are preferable.

1.3 CARDS SPEAK

"Cards speak" is poker-talk shorthand for the longer "The cards speak for themselves." Poker is predicated on the assumption that the best hand will win the pot. That means when cards are turned over at the showdown, it's no longer one player per hand when it comes to reading and determining the best hand. Though it is always up to the dealer to determine the winning hand—or winning hands in a high-low split game—dealers are human and mistakes are made. Brains lock up from time to time, even for experienced players and dealers, and each player at the table has an ethical responsibility to speak up in order to ensure that the winning hand takes the money, even if the player holding that hand overlooks it.

Mistakes don't happen all that often in Texas hold'em games, but Omaha eight-or-better-high-low-split (which we'll mercifully abbreviate from this point forward as

Omaha/8) is a game where even the best of dealers are sometimes guilty of misreading a hand. Regardless of the game, however, it is the hand itself that determines who wins the pot, not the statements of players (or even a mistaken dealer) about which hand they believe is the best one.

Moreover, you are not breaking any code of silence or other unwritten rules, and you are surely not ratting out another player by chirping up when you see a pot about to be incorrectly awarded. Poker has a long-standing tradition of being referred to as a "gentleman's game," and this directive is that tradition brought to life.

In casinos, public card rooms, and in online poker, games are always based on the fact that "cards speak." "Declare" games, never found in these public venues, are home games in which players, at the end of the hand, must *declare* whether they are betting on a high hand, a low hand, or both.

In most declare games if you state you are going both ways, you must win—or at least tie—for the best hand in each direction in order to take any portion of the pot. In other words, if I'm playing Omaha/8 and declare that I'm going both high and low, I must turn over the best high and low hand in order to take any portion of the pot. If I declare both high and low, but lose one end of the pot, my entire hand—high hand and low hand too—is null and void, and I am ineligible to win either end of the pot.

A simultaneous showing of chips or coins in each player's hand is the most commonly used method of declaration. After the cards are all out, no chips in hand usually means low, one means high, while two chips designates a hand declared in both directions. If everyone declares high, the best high hand wins the entire pot; there is no low hand.

If everyone declares low, the best low hand wins everything. If you declare both ways you will generally win or lose the entire pot. The only exception occurs when two or more hands are tied in one direction.

Again, you'll never find a declare game in a casino. They are too rife with arguments and dissent, and because "cards speak" provides an authoritative philosophy for awarding the pot to the best hand, poker has evolved in that direction. Declare games also slow down the action, which, in turn, can reduce either the rake or the number of hands played in a given collection period.

Even in home games, cards speak most of the time. The only time they don't is in a game using declarations, and then it's still a case of cards speaking, but only after the holder of those cards has declared in one or more directions.

You now have the explanation behind poker's two prime directives. With these two directives firmly in mind, and a goal to make rulings in such a way that they are consistent with the traditions of poker and the spirit of the game, firm and fair decisions can be made. The two prime directives can be joined with two other guidelines to form the foundation for any well-run game:

- ✓ One player per hand
- ✓ Cards speak
- ✓ Rule in keeping with the spirit of the game
- ✓ Rule with the traditions of poker in mind

Each is vital to poker, and collectively they provide a cohesive way to think about a fair and equitable poker environment. Use them to build a solid template for approaching poker decisions, poker rules, and the game's unwritten code of ethics.

1.4 LOCATION: CULTURAL AND REGIONAL DIFFERENCES

Although the world becomes a smaller place with each passing day, there are still significant cultural differences from one country to another, and these differences often appear as part of poker etiquette when you travel to distant locales. We Americans are fond of trash-talking our opponents, but in England no one makes a peep during the play of a hand. It's as quiet as the gallery around the green when a golfer lines up a potential winning putt at the final hole.

Cultural differences do play a role in poker. And because poker is now a worldwide game, these differences sometimes cause conflict. In most tournaments and cash games in English-speaking countries, English is the only language permitted at the poker table. If you're in a multilingual country, a nation where English is not the official language but is spoken by the majority of the population as a second language, you're likely to hear two or more languages spoken at the poker table.

It makes for an interesting way to learn the language. But sometimes poker phrases are not translated from English to other languages so much as they are "transliterated" in much the same way as "baseball" in Latin America is "beisbol." So in Austria, for example, when you make a straight, it's called a "strasse," which is the German word for "street." Why "street"? I suppose because it sounds like "straight."

They also say "flesh" for "flush." And if you remember

that song from the Rodgers and Hammerstein musical *South Pacific,* "There Is Nothing Like a Dame," in German a pair of queens are called "damen." It's not quite as regal sounding as queens, but it's two women nevertheless.

If you're in Costa Rica, lose your buy-in during a tournament and want to rebuy, just shout out "camisa." It's the Spanish for "shirt," as in, "I lost my shirt." You can also shout out "rebuy," and they'll understand what you mean, but somehow "camisa!" has a much more picturesque ring to it.

1.5 LANGUAGES PERMITTED AT POKER TABLE

Speaking a foreign language during a hand of poker is not allowed, unless expressly permitted.

INTERPRETATION NOTE

This is referred to as the "English only" rule in English speaking countries. In countries where English is not the official language, the native language is the official table language, though it is common in many European countries to permit both the native language and English at the poker table. Where a country is officially multilingual, all official languages are permissible at the table and other languages—English among them—may be permitted as local custom dictates.

1.6 THE MANAGEMENT FRAMEWORK: DECISIONS, POLICIES, AND ETIQUETTE

Before actually implementing any specific poker rule, it's important to let players know that their play, behavior, deportment, and conduct are covered by a set of rules. Not only do these rules govern the game itself, they also establish the atmosphere in which the game is played and outline a set of expectations that players, dealers, and management alike are expected to follow.

1.7 FAIR RULES: PUBLICATION AND PLAYER ENTITLEMENT

Every player is entitled to a set of rules that is both consistent in meaning and applied with fairness. Establishing an environment that provides a fair and safe game for everyone should be one of management's primary goals, whether management happens to be the corporate structure of a casino or an informal gathering of friends who play poker once a week in someone's home, in charity events, in the fraternity house, in the golf club, or in a small, neighborhood card room.

Management's primary responsibility is to protect players and the game's integrity through the fair application of rules that are consistent with the spirit and traditions of poker.

This tale was provided by Donna Marks, poker dealer.

TOPIC
Who Should Be Punished, the Dealer or the Player?

It was the early 1980s. I was sitting in a high-limit, heads-up draw game. At the time, our policy was to shuffle and then place the deck in front of the player for him or her to cut. I did so and waited. The player didn't act. He was in a conversation and very 'coked up.' He was well known for being on drugs, but he was a very good customer. After waiting a fair amount of time, I tapped the table slightly. To my shock, the customer picked the deck up and very heavily threw the deck in my face; then he yelled for another dealer!

Now the question is, when the manager comes over, does he bar the player, or take the dealer out on the customer's request?

In this situation, the customer got his way. I was taken out, crying I might add, as he seriously hurt my face. Another dealer was brought in. Although money is the club's main concern, actions like this should penalize the customer; after all, he'll be back (and will probably act up again). But the house must stick up for the dealer. I feel the situation was handled totally wrong.

1.8 EMPLOYEE AND MANAGEMENT ACCOUNTABILITY

Employees are accountable for running games in accordance with the rules and poker's prime directives. In case of a disagreement among players, the dealer's responsibility is to call for a floor supervisor to render a timely decision. The floor supervisor is responsible for decisions based on the facts and surrounding circumstances, and for interpreting rules in a manner in keeping with the principles of fairness and the traditions of poker.

While a supervisor's ruling should be rendered before the shuffle begins for the next hand, a new hand may be started at the supervisor's discretion in order to provide time to find and determine the facts. This typically occurs when facts are determined by reviewing security tapes. In that case, the pot in dispute is held in "escrow" by the floor supervisor until all the facts have been gathered and a decision is rendered.

INTERPRETATION NOTE

Inadvertent errors should be resolved with greater tolerance than deliberate violations. Supervisors should give inexperienced players more leeway than experienced and knowledgeable players. While it may not always be the case, supervisors have the latitude to presume that higher limit players are more experienced and knowledgeable about the game than players who are in lower limit games.

1.9 DECISIONS MADE BY FLOOR SUPERVISORS, NOT DEALERS

Floor supervisors, not dealers, should make all decisions involving an interpretation of rules, or decisions that involve a determination of facts and circumstances prior to applying a rule. The dealer is responsible for describing the facts to a floor supervisor, and should call upon affected

INTERPRETATION NOTE

Supervisors should be looking for facts when questioning the dealer and players. Supervisors should not rely on the dealer or players for opinions regarding interpretation of the rules, only for the facts that may lead to a ruling. When making a ruling the supervisor should state what his ruling is, and explain the ruling that supports his decision.

Should a situation arise that is not covered by these rules, the supervisor should examine the facts and render a decision that is fair, and in keeping with the best interests of the game and the traditions of poker.

In examining facts and circumstances, supervisors may determine that a player tried to take unfair advantage of another and should be disciplined. The supervisor may then warn the offending player, remove him or her from the game for a specific duration of time, suspend the player from the card room for a specific period of time, or bar the player from the card room.

players to present any information they believe will help in rendering a proper and fair decision. If facts remain in dispute, the floor supervisor may ask any players seated in the game to clarify the situation. The supervisor may also opt to review any evidence stored on security cameras.

1.10 DECISIONS MADE IN BEST INTERESTS OF GAME

Whenever a narrowly construed (letter-of-the-law) decision yields an unfair result, or a result not in keeping with the spirit behind that law, the best interests of the game, or the traditions of poker, the supervisor charged with rendering a decision may waive the rule and render a decision yielding a fair result. If one rule is in apparent conflict with another, the floor supervisor called upon to render the decision must resolve the conflict in the direction that preserves the best interests and fairness of the game.

If you're planning to use this book as your set of rules,

INTERPRETATION NOTE

The spirit of the law, the best interests of the game, and the traditions of poker are paramount, and take precedence over narrowly framed letter-of-the-law decisions. For example, the rules generally should be interpreted in such a way that the player holding the best hand is awarded the pot. This is consistent with the best interests of the game and the traditions of poker.

it's important to recognize that every player agreed to follow these rules, procedures, and standards of conduct and etiquette simply by taking a seat in the game. Every player who accepts a seat in the game accepts these rules and the authority of management to interpret them fairly, and in the best interest of poker.

Management owns the specific game being played. Therefore, management has complete discretion regarding who may play, how play is conducted, and how rules are to

---

INTERPRETATION NOTE

All of these rules are designed to be interpreted with a large measure of common sense and with the best interests of the game in mind. Applying a rule in a manner that yields an unfair result amounts to a misinterpretation of rules that should be interpreted with great latitude and in the best interests of the game, with discretion given to management in making these decisions.

Once a finding of facts has been made, the decision and interpretation of these rules rests with management, and their decisions shall be made with the best and fairest interests of the game at heart. All decisions made by management are final. Should any of these rules, regulations, or points of etiquette conflict with any applicable laws, statutes, ordinances, administrative decisions, consent decrees, or other legal findings, those rules found in conflict with the applicable legalities will be superseded.

be enforced. Management may prohibit any player from the premises or the game for any reason at all.

1.11 POLICING PLAYER CONDUCT

Management retains a number of rights that are essentially part of the terms and conditions under which games are offered to players. These rights exist in casinos, on the Internet as part of the host provider's terms of service, and in home games.

Management retains the right and authority to expel players or visitors at its discretion. Playing poker is a privilege extended by management. It is not a right that is vested in a player, customer, or visitor. By taking a seat in a game, as well as by being admitted to the facility where the game is conducted, players and visitors consent to management's at-will right to admit or eject visitors and players.

An incorrect decision made in good faith will remain in effect. Players have no recourse against management or against an employee who errs, incorrectly interprets facts, misapplies a rule, applies the wrong rule, applies a rule incorrectly, or renders a wrong decision, as long as that employee acted in good faith.

Each player or guest is responsible for his or her conduct, and each is accountable for his or her actions. Management is neither responsible for the behavior, conduct, or deportment of players or guests, nor for the conduct of employees who are not involved in the performance of their official duties. Management is responsible for employees who are performing their duties in the proscribed manner.

INTERPRETATION NOTE

Again, management runs the game and the premises where the game is held. Management has the final word on decisions, and on who may be admitted or ejected from the premises. Players are responsible for playing within the rules and for acting in accordance with poker etiquette and the traditions of the game.

1.12 INCORRECT DECISIONS MADE IN GOOD FAITH

A player has no claim against management or against any employee for a faulty decision rendered in good faith, or for any honest error by a dealer or floor supervisor.

1.13 RIGHT TO START AND BREAK GAMES

Management may start or break games at its discretion. Management may start full games or shorthanded games. Although every effort should be made to keep games going instead of breaking them, management may break games at any time, and for any reason.

1.14 RIGHT TO CHANGE GAME ELEMENTS

Management has the right to change game elements, including the betting structure, the rake, or other methods of fee collections, and may make a change any time except while

> ### INTERPRETATION NOTE
>
> No one is immune from making innocent errors and from rendering incorrect decisions. Players have no recourse against management for errors made by employees acting in good faith.
>
> The analogy that can be drawn here is that of a baseball umpire who errs in calling a runner safe when he was actually out. Although the decision may be wrong, and may be an unfortunate one, the decision will stand as long as it has been honestly rendered by an employee acting to the best of his or her ability.

a hand is in play. If any player objects to a change in betting limits, such as "converting" a $10–$20 game to one with betting limits of $15–$30, no change in stakes or other conditions should be made unless the objecting player or players can be accommodated by being moved to another table offering the same form of poker and betting limits.

1.15 RIGHT TO INTRODUCE NEW DECKS

To protect the integrity of a game, management may introduce a new deck of cards prior to the beginning of a new hand, and may also inspect any discarded hand, without regard to whether that hand was called or not.

INTERPRETATION NOTE

"Accommodated" means moving objecting players to another game of the same type, structure, and betting limits, unless the objecting players are willing to move to other games. For the purposes of accommodating another player, a $6–$12 hold'em game played with a kill is not considered identical to a $6–$12 hold'em game played without a kill.

1.16 RIGHT TO PROHIBIT CERTAIN PLAYERS FROM SAME GAME

Management has the right to prohibit players from playing in a given game and to prohibit two players from playing in the same game. Such a decision should not be construed as pejorative, but a decision to avoid even the appearance of impropriety. Management always retains the right to prohibit any player from entering or using its facilities, and may do so at will.

1.17 RIGHT TO ESTABLISH APPEARANCE AND GROOMING STANDARDS

Management has the right to establish, modify, and maintain standards for appearance, grooming, and personal hygiene, and behavior in the card room.

INTERPRETATION NOTE

To the extent possible, management should prevent husbands and wives, other family members, or those with close personal relationships from playing in the same game. Every attempt should be made to seat players with close relationships at different tables. If there are no like games available, players falling into these categories may be seated at the same table providing their relationship is made known to other players by management and no players at the table object. A new player has no right to object if he comes to the table after two players with a personal relationship have been seated in the game without objection from other players at the time they were seated.

1.18 PLAYERS-ONLY AT TABLE PROPER

A person who is not playing may not take a seat at the table itself.

1.19 GUESTS, PLAYER-SWEATING, AND SPECTATORS

In cash games, guests may sit behind players as long as no other players object, although management (at its discretion) retains the right to remove, reposition, or to otherwise restrict the spectator's view of the game. No one may sit behind another player in a tournament. Guests are expected to look only at their host's cards.

1.20 IDENTIFYING SHILLS OR PROPOSITION PLAYERS

A player paid by the house as a shill or proposition player should be identified by the dealer when entering the game.

ALTERNATE RULE: The house posts a sign advising patrons that proposition or shill players are used, but there is no requirement that they be identified when entering a game. However, if a player asks that proposition players or shills at the table be identified, the dealer must identify them. A proposition player plays with his own money and is used by management to keep games running when the card room isn't busy. A shill is used for the same purpose, but he wagers the house's money as opposed to his own. A silent proposition player is one who will not be identified as such, even if a player asks him to be identified.

ALTERNATE RULE: No *silent proposition players* are permitted.

CHAPTER 2

THE HOUSE—GAME-PLAY MANAGEMENT

Many rules are game-specific. Some apply only to tournaments or to cash games, while others are all encompassing, covering all the games that are spread in a card room. In general, these policies and procedures define and proscribe the environment in which games are played, and spell out many of the administrative procedures necessary for an efficiently functioning series of poker games.

2.1 BEGINNING NEW GAMES

To start a nine- or ten-handed game, five or more players should be present, and four players should be available to start games that are played eight-handed.

Management should make every effort to start new games, and may begin new games as either full or short games, depending on available players and projections for a game's continuity. Although short games typically won't be started with fewer than five players for nine- or ten-handed games, or four players for eight-handed games, management should make every effort to accommodate players who wish to begin games with fewer players. These extremely short games—fewer than five or four players, depending on the type of game—will not be considered *must-move* games for purposes of keeping the main game full unless they have four or five players seated.

2.2 ESTABLISHING AND MAINTAINING SEATING ORDER FOR NEW GAMES

Floor supervisors or other employees, such as *brushes* or *board attendants,* who are responsible for building and maintaining interest and preference lists for new games should call names from the list when a new game is slated to start.

Players higher on the list have priority. List placement or reservation is based on the time a player puts her name on a list, not the time the player arrives in the room.

2.3 DETERMINING BUTTON PLACEMENT IN NEW GAMES

One card is dealt to each seated player at the table whenever a new game begins. The high card by suit is awarded the button, and the blinds will begin with the two players seated to the immediate left of the button. The order of suits are, in reverse alphabetical order, from highest to lowest: spades, hearts, diamonds, clubs, thus making the ace of spades the highest card in the deck for this purpose.

Once shuffling commences for the first hand, any player who did not participate in the draw is required to post blinds if he takes a seat that has already been passed at least once by the dealer button. His options are to wait for the blinds to reach him, in which case he shall be required to post a big blind, then a small blind in turn. He may also wait for the button to pass his seat and post one big blind in order to receive a hand.

A player taking a seat to the left of the blind on the first orbit of a new game (the button has not yet passed the new player's seat) is entitled to a hand. He then must post his blinds in turn.

When approved by the floor supervisor, the dealer should begin shuffling when six players are seated and have chips in their possession in nine- or ten-handed games, and when five players are seated in games that are dealt eight-handed. Any players who arrive after the cards are shuffled but prior to the blinds passing their seat will receive a free hand just as if they had been seated at the table when the game began. If the blind has passed the seat of a new player, he will be treated as a new player in an existing game, and is required to either post a single, live, big blind after the button passes his seat, or wait for his turn in the big blind before receiving a hand.

Although it is generally forbidden, some casinos allow players who have missed posting their blinds to "buy the button" in flop games such as hold'em and Omaha. Buying the button occurs when a player returns to the table after missing both blinds but before the button has passed his or her seat. To buy the button, the player posts one live big blind and one dead small blind when in the small blind position. The button remains with the player who last had it. On the next hand, the player buying the button gets the button and the players who were to have been the blinds in the previous hand will now post their blinds as usual. No one misses any blind, and no one pays extra blinds when a player buys the button.

2.4 PLAYERS' SELECTION OF SEATS IN NEW GAMES

A player may designate her seat preference for any seats not already spoken for when she puts her name on a waiting list for a new game. When the new game begins, the floor supervisor responsible for starting that game shall ensure that the integrity of the seating order is maintained. Once the first hand is dealt, anyone who indicated a seat preference but failed to lock up her seat at the table loses her priority on the waiting list.

Any player who is active in another game may *lock up* a seat in the new game, under these conditions:

- ✓ He may lock up a seat until his hand ends.
- ✓ If he has paid at least one of his blinds, he may lock up his seat until after playing the button.

In any event, if the blinds pass him in the new game, he will be given a missed blind button and is required to post one big blind after the button passes his seat or wait until it is his turn in the big blind before he is dealt a hand.

ALTERNATE RULE: Table seats are based on arrival at the table after being called to the new game. This *first come, first served* seating philosophy will be operative regardless of a player's place on the game's waiting list. If two players arrive at the same time, they draw for the seat.

2.5 PUTTING DECKS IN PLAY IN NEW GAMES

A dealer at a new game is required to spread the suited deck on the table so that all new players can see that the deck is complete. Both the front of the deck and the back

INTERPRETATION NOTE

We much prefer seat choices based on preference designation at the time a player's name is added to the waiting list. The "land rush" method is frequently fraught with "I was here first" arguments that are unnecessary.

are spread. Each card is accounted for and the dealer also determines that all of the cards have the same back pattern. She will not begin scrambling and shuffling until told to by the floor supervisor who is accountable for the new game. In most games, a new dealer is introduced every half hour, and the new dealer changes decks. Changing decks is not introducing a "new" deck.

2.6 TIME REQUIRED BETWEEN DECK CHANGES

When a deck change is requested and introduced into a game, the newly introduced deck shall be used for at least one full orbit of the table, unless it is inadvertently damaged. A brand-new deck must be used until the regularly scheduled deck change, unless defective or damaged.

2.7 MINIMUM AND MAXIMUM BUY-IN REQUIREMENTS FOR NEW GAMES

Each player at a new game must have chips or cash in front of him equal to the game's minimum buy-in, or have chips in transit. Playing with chips in transit is dependent upon the player having given at least the minimum buy-in for that game to a floor supervisor or chip attendant, and having the dealer announce the amount he is *playing behind*. [See Rule 2.44.]

A player arriving at a new game with less than the minimum buy-in shall not be dealt in and is not eligible for a short buy-in.

Some no-limit games have a maximum buy-in as well as a minimum. Any player with fewer than the maximum allowable number of chips may rebuy, but only to the maximum limit.

2.8 PROCEDURES FOR PLAYER WISHING TO CHANGE SEATS IN SAME GAME

A seated player always has preference over a new player not yet active in the game to move to any seat that becomes vacant at that table.

Priority among players already seated at the game should be established by the order in which players request a seat change. Seat-change buttons designated "first seat change," "second seat change," and "third seat change" should be used to keep track of player preference as seats become vacant and available at a table.

A player with seat-change priority may accept or pass any available seat that becomes vacant. If the player with first priority passes, the second player on the list has the right to accept or reject the available seat.

ALTERNATE RULE: A player who requested but doesn't take an available seat change loses her priority and will be placed at the bottom of the seat-change list.

INTERPRETATION NOTE

An outgoing dealer should advise the incoming dealer of any pending seat-change requests. If no seat-change requests are pending, the dealer should ask if anyone wants to move to a vacant seat before seating a new player from the game's waiting list.

Once a request has been processed, the player who just changed seats goes to the back of the list. Any new players should rank behind an existing player who just made a seat change and moved down the list.

Disputes in seniority can be resolved by having players draw for available seats, but using seat-change buttons can prevent all of these issues.

2.9 SEAT CHANGES IN GAMES WITH BLINDS: SITTING OUT HANDS

If a player changes seats at the same table, the following standards apply:

- ✓ For moving to adjacent, unoccupied seats: The seat change is transparent to the flow of the game and is allowed at will.
- ✓ For moving counterclockwise (toward the blinds and against the flow of the dealer button), jumping over intermediate players to the new seat: There is no penalty for changing seats and the player who moves is entitled to receive a hand immediately.

✓ For moving clockwise (away from the blinds and in the same direction as the flow of the dealer button): The player is required to sit out a number of hands equal to the number of players jumped over during the move. As an example, suppose the button is at Seat 1, and a player in Seat 6 requests a move to Seat 9, the only vacant seat at the table. In this instance, the moving player would be required to sit out two hands, because he has jumped over two players (Seats 7 and 8). It is the dealer's responsibility to track the number of seats moved and the number of hands sat out by the moving player before he is allowed to rejoin play. If the player does not wish to wait out any hands, he may be dealt in immediately, provided he posts the big blind in his new seat.

INTERPRETATION NOTE

In practice, same-table seat changes work easiest when a player deals off by moving from the button seat to another vacant seat, because any move that he makes is considered a move toward the blinds (counterclockwise). Because of this, the moving player is not required to sit out any hands, and play can continue unimpeded.

At a full table, moving from a seat currently in one of the blinds is not allowed.

ALTERNATE RULE: Some casinos allow players to move out of the small blind and post it live in another seat. This does give the player better position, but the compensation is that the player is deprived of the right to play the button on the next hand.

2.10 SEAT CHANGES IN GAMES WITH BLINDS: OTHER REQUIREMENTS

Any player who pays her blinds has the right to deal off before changing seats, whether to a vacant seat at the same table or a new table altogether. If a new player is waiting to take her seat and is willing to post a big blind behind the button, or is otherwise entitled to a free hand, the player dealing off must change seats immediately after she deals off.

If the new player is unwilling to post behind the button and is not entitled to receive a free hand, the player who is changing seats may keep his existing seat until it is his turn to post the big blind in his new seat.

If an incoming player declares he will not post behind the button, she cannot change his mind if that would require the player who is changing seats to move before he is required to post the big blind.

2.11 PERMISSION REQUIRED TO JOIN EXISTING GAMES

Permission is required before taking a seat in a game. In large casinos and card rooms, this permission is secured from a board attendant or "brush" person, while in smaller card rooms permission will be secured from a floor supervisor or the dealer.

2.12 PROCEDURES GOVERNING NEW
PLAYER'S SEAT SELECTION

No new player should be given any options or choices regarding seat selection before existing players have acted on those same options. When a new player has locked up a seat, has chips down or has chips in transit, she is considered to be an existing player.

New players may not sit down without first obtaining permission from the dealer or the floor supervisor. With their consent, the new player may lock up or otherwise occupy a seat.

Prior to assigning a seat to a new player, the dealer should inquire as to whether any existing player wishes that seat if there are no seat-change buttons to be processed.

A seat is not considered occupied or locked up without a floor supervisor's or dealer's permission. Once the dealer queries existing players about their interest in the vacant seat and the new player takes that seat, it is no longer considered to be an open seat, nor available as a transfer destination for an existing player.

2.13 WAITING LISTS

Any player called for an existing game should take or lock up his seat immediately. The sole exception is if the player called has paid the big blind at his current table, in which case he may play his small blind and then deal off before moving to another game.

A player in this situation should notify the floor supervisor, board attendant, or brush that he is in the blinds and planning to deal off before moving. The floor supervisor or dealer will then lock up that seat for the player, with the lockup remaining valid until that player deals off. Once he deals off, he must move into the new game promptly, or lose his rights to the new seat.

Any player who does not promptly take a seat when called will be rolled to the bottom of the waiting list.

A player who is given an electronic notification device has five minutes from the time she is notified to come to the poker room and take her seat. If she is not present in the poker room after that period, her seat will be given to the next player on the list. A player who does not respond to her electronic notification within five minutes will be rotated to the end of the list.

Players must be in the poker room to be placed on a waiting list. Phone-ins and e-mails are not permissible.

ALTERNATE RULE 1: Guests in the casino's hotel may phone in from their rooms to be placed on a poker waiting list.

ALTERNATE RULE 2: Phoning in to be placed on a poker waiting list is permissible.

2.14 RESERVING SEATS WHILE ON WAITING LISTS

A player may leave *lock-up money* with a floor supervisor. The lock-up amount should be twenty dollars ($20) or one small betting unit, whichever is larger.

A player who locks up a seat but does not return in time to post the big blind will be given a "missed blind" button. If he fails to return to a time collection game when his seat rental is due, collection will be taken from his lock-up deposit. The floor supervisor will hold the remainder of the deposit for any player failing to claim his seat within thirty minutes of reserving it with the lockup, and will return this deposit remainder to the player when he arrives. The next player on the waiting list will be given the seat after the thirty minutes have elapsed.

ALTERNATE RULE: Players may not reserve a seat by leaving lock-up money with the floor supervisor. To claim a seat, a player must be in the room to take her seat when paged, or within five minutes if the room uses electronic paging devices to notify players that their seat is available.

2.15 PLAYERS REQUESTING TABLE CHANGES

Floor supervisors are responsible for making and retaining lists for players wishing to transfer to another table of the same game and stakes. Transfers are made as seats become available, by priority of the request.

Players may not transfer from one game to another without permission of the floor supervisor. Unless he is entering from a broken game (which is not considered a table change), no player may be seated at a new table unless he has the minimum buy-in for that game. A player from a broken game may be seated at another table with the chips he has in play at the time his game broke. [For minimum chip requirements when changing tables, see Rule 2.45.]

ALTERNATE RULE 1: A player may change tables with the chips he has in play, even if that amount is insufficient to comprise a minimum buy-in for that game.

INTERPRETATION NOTE

If a player transfers from a \$10–\$20 hold'em game played with a kill, to a \$10–\$20 hold'em game played without a kill, those games are considered to be different games for purposes of determining the minimum buy-in. A player transferring from a kill game to a game at the same stakes without a kill—or vice versa—must have the minimum buy-in as a requirement for entering the new game.

Transferring is not permitted if it would cause the transferee's table to have fewer players than the game she is transferring into.

ALTERNATE RULE 2: Transferring is permitted as long as there is no net difference in table composition.

INTERPRETATION NOTE

If one table is six-handed and another seven-handed, a transfer from the seven-handed to the six-handed game is permissible, but a transfer from the six-handed game to the seven-handed game is forbidden.

Table transfers are not permitted when *must-move* rules are in effect. [See Rule 2.18].

2.16 BREAKING GAMES

If players are willing to play shorthanded, games with three players or fewer should not be broken. However, a player should not be required to play in a four- or five-handed game that is normally dealt eight- or nine-handed.

If players are unwilling to play five- or four-handed, the floor supervisor will break the game and give existing players an opportunity to join another game of the same type and wagering limits.

ALTERNATE RULE: If a majority of players at the table wish to break a five- or four-handed game and sufficient seats are available in other games of the same type and limits, the game may be broken at the discretion of the floor supervisor.

2.17 SEATING PLAYERS FROM BROKEN GAMES

Determining the seating order for open seats is done by drawing cards among players coming from a broken game. Players draw cards, and those able to be seated in existing games will be accommodated. If there are more players than available seats, the floor supervisor establishes a waiting list based on the draw.

A player entering a game of the same type and limits as a broken game is not required to post a blind in order to receive a hand, nor is she required to have the minimum buy-in to take a seat at the new table. If the broken game was a kill game and the new game does not have a kill, they are considered different games for purposes of determining the buy-in requirements.

INTERPRETATION NOTE

If a player in a $6–$12 game that breaks is seated in another $6–$12 game, she shall be dealt in immediately, without regard to whether she has taken her blind at the new table. She does not need to post behind the button to receive a hand. The only exception is that a transferring player may not take a seat between the blinds, or on the button.

In addition, there is no requirement for a player to have the minimum buy-in when leaving a broken game and transferring to another game of the same type and betting limits. A player leaving a broken game is treated as though she were an existing player at the new game, so long as the game type and betting limits are the same.

If a player is moved from a broken $10–$20 hold'em game played with a kill to a $10–$20 hold'em game played without a kill—or vice versa—she is considered to be moving to a different game for the purpose of determining the minimum buy-in. A player moved from a broken kill game to a game at the same stakes without a kill—or vice versa—must have the minimum buy-in as a requirement for entering the new game.

Any absent players from the broken game will be added to the waiting list as they return to the game area. If more than one game is available at the limits of the broken game, the player drawing the high card by suit has first choice of seating. Seat selection for players coming from a broken game will be made after any players on a transfer list from existing games or players who requested a seat change have exercised their options.

> ### INTERPRETATION NOTE
>
> If a player has been gone from the table for only a short time, as would be the case if he took a bathroom break, he will be treated as though he was not away from the table. This determination should be made at the floor supervisor's discretion.

ALTERNATE RULE: A list of players from a broken game will take precedence over a transfer list.

2.18 ESTABLISHING AND ADMINISTERING *MUST-MOVE* GAMES

To protect an existing game or games, a *must-move* or *forced-move* game may be established. A must-move list is maintained as though it were a waiting list, and players will be moved from the forced-move game to the main game as seats in the main game become available.

ALTERNATE RULE: If a player would prefer to remain in the must-move game, the floor supervisor will ask for volunteers to transfer to the main game, and select players for the main game in the same order in which they appear on the must-move list.

If no volunteers can be found for the main game, the floor supervisor will move the player at the top of the must-move list into the main game. If a mandatory move is required and a player refuses to go, she will be removed from the must-move game and will not be permitted to play in a game of that type and limits for two hours.

INTERPRETATION NOTE

If Paulie is first up on the list to move to the main game but would prefer to stay in the must-move game, the floor supervisor will ask for volunteers to go to the main game. If both Tony and Junior wish to go to the main game, the floor supervisor shall seat whichever player is closer to the top of the must-move list.

When a must-move game is established, players will be seated in order of their place on the waiting list. Players not taking a seat promptly in the must-move game will be rotated to the back of the waiting list. Lock-up procedures will be followed for must-move games, as will procedures covering the seating of players who have been given electronic paging devices.

A must-move player is not required to have the minimum buy-in for the main game, so long as he brings all of his chips with him and does not take money off the table when moving from a forced-move game to the main game.

A player who enters the main game from a must-move game is not required to post a blind before receiving a hand, but he will not be permitted to join the main game between the blinds or on the button.

A player moving to the main game is expected to do so expeditiously and may not play to his blinds. However, if he has posted his big blind, he may deal off and then move.

Players in a shorthanded must-move game are required to keep playing to retain their spot on the must-move list. If they opt not to play shorthanded—unless the game is less than five- or four-handed in games that are traditionally nine- or ten-handed (such as hold'em), or eight-handed (such as stud)—they will be rolled to the bottom of the must-move list and will not be seated in the main game until after all players in the must-move game are seated in the main game.

Any player who is absent when it is her turn to move will not have the opportunity to refuse the move and will be placed in the main game. The floor supervisor is accountable for counting the absent player's chips, announcing the total to the dealer and the table, and moving those chips to the open seat at the main game.

Missed-blind and absent buttons will accompany the player to the main game. However, if he is absent when seated at the main game, but would otherwise have been the *third man walking* at the main game, he will not be designated as a third man walking until he can be notified of that status. Under these circumstances, a fourth player who gets up from the table will be designated as the third man walking. [See Rule 2.34.]

If a third game of the same type and limits begins, it will also become a must-move game, and the moving sequence will involve players moving from the second game into the main game and from the third game into the second. However, if no one from the second game wishes to move into the main game, then third-game players will be afforded an opportunity to move to the main game and mandatory moves into both the main and second games will come from the third game.

With more than three games of the same type and limit, the first game started and second game will be main games. Players from the third and fourth games will fill available seats in the first two games, and seat-transfer requests between the first two games will be honored prior to filling vacancies.

A game that has been running for two hours is no longer considered a must-move game and will be a main game on equal footing with any other main games with the same game type and wagering limits.

Players are not permitted to transfer from a main game into a forced-move feeder game.

2.19 TIME COLLECTIONS

The two predominant methods of collecting revenue from poker games are raking each pot [see Rule 2.20] and charging time collection, which amounts to a rental charge for playing in the game. Time collections are made every half hour, in advance, whereas rakes involve removing a token sum up to a specified maximum from each pot.

The choice of which method to exercise is usually based on tradition, although sometimes governmental regulation or law either proscribes or prohibits one or another method. For example, California law prohibits the house from having any interest in the pot, so raking is not permitted.

Each player pays a time collection to the dealer, usually

every half hour or each time a new dealer enters the box. This fee—in essence a rental fee for the chair, table, cards, dealers, chips, light, heat, power, and other utilities—is always paid in advance.

A typical time charge might be $8 per half hour for a $20–$40 game, with lower rates for games with smaller betting units, and a higher rake for bigger games.

The time collection procedure is simple and straightforward. When due, the dealer announces that he is *taking collection*. Each player posts the amount to be collected in front of him. The dealer collects it, beginning with the player on his left and working his way around the table. The dealer takes collection from all players, including those who are away from the table.

Any new player joining a game within five minutes following time collection is required to pay a time charge, although if the game is not full and there is no waiting list, the floor supervisor may choose to forgo a payment from new players.

In any event, a player who joins a game more than five minutes after collections will not have to pay until the next collection period. Time charges are not prorated.

If a game breaks up within fifteen minutes following collection, the most recent time charge should be refunded.

2.20 RAKED POTS

Though not a legal method of charging players in California, raking the pot is the most commonly employed method in Nevada casinos. A typical rake is 5 or 10 percent of the pot, up to a maximum of $3 or $4, though in some locations the maximum rake can be as high as $10.

INTERPRETATION NOTE

At the house's discretion, a player who declines to pay the collection may play one more hand in a stud game, or may play until his or her blind in button games, as long as no one is waiting for a seat in the game.

If two or more players are on a list when the collection becomes due, everyone is required to pay collection. New players do not have to pay collection as long as there is no more than one person waiting.

The amount raked from the pot is predicated on the size of the pot. Side pots are included for purposes of calculating the rake. The rake, however, is always taken from the main pot, never from the side pot.

Once awarded, a dealer may not take additional rake from a pot, even if she erred initially in calculating the correct amount. If the dealer rakes too much from the pot, it should be corrected if pointed out before the next hand is dealt.

2.21 TIME POTS

This collection method has fallen out of favor in many areas; it involves a collection taken from the next one or two pots won after time payments are due. In a *time pot,* the hands' winners pay all the time for the players at the table who have voluntarily agreed to participate in the time pot.

One reason this method has fallen out of favor is that it severely constrains action, with players understandably unwilling to risk money to win a pot that will go, in large part, to the casino. Also, because it's based on an honor system and the floor cannot enforce time pot collections,

INTERPRETATION NOTE

Rather than having the entire time collection paid by the winner of the next hand, some time pots are administered by dividing the payment over the next two hands that reach a predetermined threshold.

For example, in a $20–$40 hold'em game where the time collection is $8 per half hour, the time collection for a full, nine-handed game would be $72. If Sally agrees to administer the time pot, she will pay time charges to the dealer for the entire table when they are due. She will be reimbursed by the winner of each of the next two pots that total at least $360. The winner of each of those pots will pay her $36 (10 percent of the pot), thus allowing Sally to recover the time collection fees that she "advanced" on behalf of the players at the table.

The administration of time pots is a player-determined process, and management has no responsibility for ensuring that these advances and reimbursements are handled appropriately. Any player at the table who does not want to participate in a time pot may opt out by paying her time charge directly. This will reduce the amount of money collected by the player administering the time pot accordingly.

players who front the time pot for other players sometimes lose money from players who play a hand or two and then get up without fulfilling their obligation to pay time. On the plus side, it saves time and allows more hands to be played in a situation where time—literally—is money. And it favors tight players who involve themselves in fewer pots.

ALTERNATE RULE: The dealer collects from players not present at the table, thereby reducing the amount taken from the time pot.

2.22 COLLECTING ON BUTTON

In these games, which are rare, the player on the button posts an amount of money to be collected in lieu of either a time charge or a rake. Money posted on the button is generally considered *live* in low-limit games, but is *dead* in games played at higher limits.

Because no button is used in stud games, collection is taken from the antes. If a flop game ends before the flop is dealt, no collection is taken. If no card is dealt on fourth street in a stud game, no collection is taken. If a player is absent when it is his turn to post a button collection, the dealer takes the appropriate sum from the player's stack and places it in the pot. It is considered dead money.

2.23 CASH ON TABLE

Cash is permitted on the table, but should be changed into chips at the dealer's earliest convenience for use in play. Only $100 bills are permitted to play. [See Rule 2.24.] Lesser-denomination bills must be changed into chips in order to be wagered. [See Rule 3.30.]

INTERPRETATION NOTE

Chips make it easier for the dealer to ensure that the pot is correct. Using chips instead of cash also makes it easier for players to determine approximately how much opponents have in front of them. Because it can be important to know how much an opponent has available to play, it is important and ethical for players to keep their own chips stacked neatly, and in plain sight. Doing this permits a player to count, or closely estimate, the amount of chips opponents have available for play.

For these reasons, chips are preferred over bills. If a player is unaware of this rule and attempts to play cash, the dealer may allow this as long as no other players in the pot object. If a player is permitted to play cash, he must change it into chips at the hand's conclusion. Chips from other casinos are never permitted to play.

2.24 PLAYING CASH INSTEAD OF CHIPS

Cash, other than hundred-dollar bills, does not play and is not permitted on the table in games smaller than $10–$20.

ALTERNATE RULE 1: Hundred-dollar bills play in all games.

ALTERNATE RULE 2: In games smaller than $10–$20, all cash plays.

INTERPRETATION NOTE

If differing denominations were permitted on the table, players would have no idea how much money each opponent has in play. Chips are much more easily counted than bills, and make for a faster-moving game.

2.25 CHIPS PLACED ON TABLE

Chips must be placed on the table and not played out of a rack.

INTERPRETATION NOTE

This is a rule born of tradition—chip racks are designed for chip storage and transportation, not for display and stacking of chips at the table.

Some casinos allow racks of chips on the table but require that a player have at least one "working stack" of at least twenty chips out of the rack and on the table in front of her.

2.26 CHIPS IN FULL VIEW

Players have an absolute right to know how much money every opponent at the table has in play. Consequently, all money in play shall be in full view at all time. In pot-limit and no-limit cash games and tournaments, large-denomination chips should be stacked in front so that they are not hidden from view by a player's lower-denominated chips. Before acting in pot-limit or no-limit games, a player has the right to ask the dealer to "count down" his opponent's chips.

2.27 REMOVING MONEY FROM TABLE

Money and, rarely, chips may be removed for security purposes when leaving the table, although this is not encouraged. Management is not responsible for any shortage of chips left on the table during a player's absence. Should a shortage be noticed or claimed, management will use its video security or other monitoring devices to determine the facts surrounding the allegation, thereby protecting the players to the extent that they can. Money removed from the table must be returned to the table when a player returns to the game.

ALTERNATE RULE: Money may not be removed from the table except when cashing out, other than small sums to pay for food and beverages, or to be used for tips.

2.28 RETURNING TO SAME GAME AFTER CASHING OUT

If you return to the same game within one hour of cashing out, your buy-in must be equal to or greater than the amount removed when leaving that game.

2.29 TABLE STAKES

All games are table stakes. Only the chips in front of a player at the start of a deal (or cash, where permissible) may play during that hand, with one exception: a player may *play behind* [see Rule 2.44] if he has purchased chips but a casino employee has not yet brought them to the table. The amount of chips purchased by a player must be announced to the table, or only the minimum buy-in may be played. All chips and money must be kept in plain view. Small sums may be taken from chips in play to pay for beverages, food, or tips.

INTERPRETATION NOTE

Simply put, you can't reach into your wallet for more money and you cannot purchase additional chips and put them into play in the midst of a hand. If you run out of chips, you are "all-in," and are contesting only that portion of the pot that your wagers cover.

Other active players who continue wagering are contesting a "side pot" that the all-in player is ineligible to win. If additional players go all-in on subsequent betting rounds, additional side pots are created, so that players with chips can still bet.

At the hand's conclusion, side pots are awarded first, from the most recently created side pot to the oldest. Finally, the main pot—which all players are eligible for—is awarded. At that point, players may buy chips and put them into play on the next hand.

2.30 NUMBER OF BETS AND RAISES
PERMITTED IN LIMIT GAMES

In limit poker, all games allow a maximum of a bet and four raises in pots involving three or more players.

ALTERNATE RULE: A bet and three raises is allowed.

INTERPRETATION NOTE

In California, it's usually a bet and three raises, while in Nevada it's a bet and four raises. The rule in play is generally more a function of geography than anything else.

2.31 NUMBER OF BETS AND RAISES
PERMITTED WHEN BETTING ROUND IS
HEADS-UP

There is no limit on the number of raises if only two players begin that round of wagering.

ALTERNATE RULE 1: If a betting round starts with three or more players, but is reduced to two players prior to reaching the maximum number of raises, those two remaining players may continue to wager with no limit on the number of raises.

In games with only two betting rounds (such as draw and lowball) betting is capped after a bet and six raises.

ALTERNATE RULE 2: In games with only two betting rounds (such as draw and lowball) betting is capped after a bet and four raises.

In pot-limit and no-limit, there is no cap on the number of raises.

INTERPRETATION NOTE

There's a lot of variety where this rule is concerned. Some card rooms, concerned about the possibilities of player collusion, have reduced the number of raises per round to three or four for all fixed-limit games.

2.32 OVERSIZED CHIP RULE

When blinds have been posted or other players have placed bets into the pot, and a player places a single chip or bill larger than the bet into the pot without announcing a raise, his action is considered a call. This rule also applies when more than one chip is required to call a bet, but the last chip might be viewed as a raise. When a player is the first to enter the pot with a single chip, and the amount of the bet is not structured, the denomination of the single chip shall equal the bet.

INTERPRETATION NOTE

If you want to raise, just say "raise." If you neglect to speak up, or forget to, you might forgo your opportunity.

2.33 ABSENT PLAYERS

A new dealer should place a "player absent" button in front of the seat of any player who leaves the table.

INTERPRETATION NOTE

It is common in many casinos to use two "player absent" buttons plus fifteen minutes before picking up a player's chips and filling that seat with the next player on the waiting list.

In time collection games, a charge will be taken from any player away from the table. If the player has an insufficient amount of money in his stacks to pay his time charge, his money will be picked up by the floor supervisor, held for him, and his seat awarded to the next player on the waiting list.

In most casinos, if a player returns within fifteen minutes of being picked up, he will be placed first on the waiting list for that game.

Whenever more than one player has been picked up, the first player who returns—not the first one who had his chips picked up—goes to the head of the list.

2.34 THIRD MAN WALKING

Any time two people are absent from a table, the next person to get up is given a button by the dealer and informed that he must return before his next blind or his chips will be picked up and his seat vacated and awarded to the first player on the waiting list.

ALTERNATE RULE: The absent player's chips will be used as blinds and he will not be removed from the table.

> ### INTERPRETATION NOTE
> This rule helps keep games full while allowing a player enough time for a quick restroom trip.

2.35 *PLAYING OVER* ABSENT PLAYERS

When a player plans to be away from the table for at least a half hour, the floor supervisor may permit the next player on the waiting list to *play over* the absent player, as long as the absent player has not requested that no one be permitted to play over him. No one may play over without permission from the floor supervisor. The floor supervisor will provide a "play-over box" to secure the absent player's chips. Permission from the absent player is not necessary for a play over to occur.

The absent player may request her seat back at any time and has the right to play the next hand dealt, unless the temporary player has posted a blind. In that circumstance, the temporary player is permitted to play both his blinds and deal off before surrendering his seat. The temporary player is then allowed to reclaim his original spot on the list of those waiting for games. If a seat becomes available while playing over, the temporary player moves into the available seat and is treated as a new player.

INTERPRETATION NOTE

Playing over occurs when a player is absent from the table for an extended time—usually when she informs the floor supervisor or dealer that she is going to dinner. Another player then plays over the absent player, using his own chips. The absent player's chips are protected by placing a Lucite or other clear "play-over" box over them, and the temporary player is never permitted to remove the play-over box or touch the absent player's chips.

Playing over is common in Las Vegas and other venues where food service is not available at the poker table. In California casinos and other card rooms that provide table service, players are able to order from a dinner menu and dine at the table, so playing over does not typically occur in these locations.

ALTERNATE RULE: Playing over is prohibited.

2.36 RESPONSIBILITY FOR CHIPS LEFT ON TABLES

Management is not responsible for cash or chips left on the table by players, whether or not the amount is verified by a floor supervisor or security cameras. Management also bears no responsibility for chips or money left on the table in the case of theft or natural disaster. Nevertheless, a player who wants to keep her seat at the table must leave her chips

INTERPRETATION NOTE

Because playing over creates potential security issues regarding the absent player's chips, many establishments prohibit it, believing that it's more trouble than it's worth. This concern, however, can be mitigated by having a departing player's chips counted down and recorded in the floor supervisor's notebook before he departs.

On the other hand, playing over permits more players to enter a game and keep the table full if the lists are long, and in any event, the house maximizes its earnings by keeping its tables full of paying players.

on the table. In tournaments, players are not to remove their chips from the table except when moving tables as instructed by the tournament director. [See Rules 2.27 and 10.8.]

❋❋❋❋❋❋❋❋❋❋❋

Tournament director Dave Lamb reports this story from the London Open.

TOPIC
Chip Count Irregularity: The Case of the Missing $5,000 Chip

When the final table of nine players remained, the players' chips were counted and bagged, and each player's signature verified the correct count. When the final table nine reassembled and were seated, the sealed plastic bags containing their respective chip totals were brought to them. The players opened, counted, and confirmed their own bags to verify that they contained the correct amounts before the play resumed.

On the occasion in question, as the players opened and counted their chips, the tournament director and several players heard a chip bounce on the table's surface.

When the players recounted their chips, the short-stack at the table, who was supposed to have three $5,000 chips and one $1,000 chip, discovered he now had just two $5,000 chips and one $1,000 chip. He was missing a $5,000 chip, a third of his total.

The players were asked to vacate the table and each player's chips were counted and found to be correct. The missing $5,000 chip did not end up in front of another player. The entire area was carefully combed; floor, rails, chairs, and even the pants cuffs of players were searched. No $5,000 chip was found.

Decision

After some delay and with all apparent avenues investigated, the game was ordered to resume. Because the chip totals had been counted, recounted, and verified by all players at every stage of the process, it was finally decided to proceed with the short-stack playing without the $5,000 chip. The decision to continue without the missing chip was predicated on the principle that once a player signs for and takes possession of his or her chips, they become the player's responsibility.

Fortunately, just as play was to resume, the short-stack found the missing $5,000 chip in the breast pocket of his jacket, which he had hung on the back of his chair. Unseen by anyone, the $5,000 chip bounced off the table and into the player's pocket.

2.37 PICKING UP ABSENT PLAYER'S CHIPS

A player's chips may be picked up if he is away from the table for more than thirty minutes. Absences may be extended by notifying a floor supervisor. However, recurring absences are grounds for a floor supervisor to pick up an absent player's chips and award that seat to the first player on the game's waiting list.

INTERPRETATION NOTE

An absence of more than thirty minutes typically occurs when a player intends to go to dinner, and forty-five minutes is the typical time allowed for a dinner break.

2.38 PUSHING ANTES

Posting an ante (also called "pushing antes") with another player is not allowed.

INTERPRETATION NOTE

Even if this is done with the most innocent of intentions, such as to prevent a temporary playing-behind situation, pushing antes gives the illusion that two players are colluding, and is not permitted for that reason.

2.39 CHOPPING BLINDS

In cash games, chopping the big and small blind by taking them back when all other players have folded is allowed in button games. Once there is any action whatsoever, splitting pots is not permitted. In tournament play, chopping blinds is not permitted. See Rule 9.45.

2.40 DIVIDING ODD CHIPS

When dividing an uneven pot results in a leftover or "odd" chip, it should be distributed as follows:

✓ To the nearest player contesting the pot to the left of the dealer button
✓ To the high card by suit in high-hand stud games
✓ To the low card by suit in low stud games such as razz
✓ To the winner of the high hand in high-low split games

In the event of multiple odd chips when three or more players chop the pot, the odd chips are distributed in order to participating players beginning to the left of the dealer button. For purposes of dividing odd chips, chips shall be broken down only to the lowest-limit chip generally used for that game.

INTERPRETATION NOTE

In a $20–$40 hold'em game, chips shall not be broken down to increments smaller than five-dollar chips. But in a $20-$40 seven-stud/8 game, where dollar chips are used for the bring-in bet, chip divisions shall be made in one-dollar increments.

2.41 RABBIT HUNTING

The practice of looking through the discards or deck stub, usually referred to as *rabbit hunting*, is not permitted, and dealers should refrain from showing cards that would have been dealt to any players.

2.42 MINIMUM AND MAXIMUM BUY-INS

The minimum buy-in for a game should not be less that ten times the small bet in fixed-limit games. In pot-limit or no-limit games, the minimum buy-in should not be less than twenty times the big blind. The house may also establish a maximum buy-in for these games.

2.43 SHORT BUY-INS

Only one "short buy-in" per session is permitted. A short buy-in occurs when a player has no more chips—typically

INTERPRETATION NOTE

These rules apply upon entering a game, purchasing more chips after going all-in and losing, or rejoining a game within an hour of leaving. (Rejoining a game within an hour of leaving is considered the same playing session.)

after going all-in and losing—and purchases a number of chips that are too few to afford him the minimum buy-in for that game.

ALTERNATE RULE: A short buy-in occurs when a player has fewer chips than the minimum buy-in required and purchases additional chips, but his total chip count when newly purchased chips are added to his existing chips still fails to meet the minimum buy-in

2.44 PLAYING BEHIND

Additional chips or money may not be introduced into the game during active play of a hand. To prevent this situation from occuring and to speed overall play, a player may *play behind* when he has provided money to a chip attendant or floor supervisor for the purchase of chips.

The player buying additional chips must announce to the dealer the amount that he is playing behind. The dealer then announces this to the rest of the table. If a player gives money to a chip attendant or floor supervisor for purchasing chips from the cashier, that employee is required to tell

INTERPRETATION NOTE

The alternate rule triggers a short buy-in whenever a player buys fewer chips than are needed to provide him with the aggregate number of chips to meet the minimum buy-in for that game.

The more common rule is predicated on a player going all-in and losing, then buying less than the game's minimum requirement. While your authors prefer the alternate rule, the rule that requires a player to go broke in a hand and then re-buy for less than the game minimum in order to trigger the short buy-in rule is far more common.

A player who re-buys after having made a short buy-in must purchase the minimum number of chips required or surrender his seat if there is a waiting list.

If there is no waiting list, a player may make more than one short buy-in as long as there are no objections from other players. A player who is not all-in may add chips to his stack in any denomination at any time before the beginning of the following hand's deal. If he adds fewer chips than those required for a minimum buy-in, it does not trigger the short buy-in rule.

the dealer the player's seat number and the amount he is *playing behind.*

Playing behind is allowed for the amount of chips that a player has purchased and which are in transit. The amount

THE HOUSE—GAME-PLAY MANAGEMENT

INTERPRETATION NOTE

A player without chips must produce the amount he is playing behind in order to be dealt a hand. Whenever someone plays behind, chips equivalent to his action are pulled from the pot by the dealer and placed in front of him each time he bets, calls, or raises. This provides a correct accounting of the money he owes to the winner of the pot.

in play must be announced to the table, or only the amount of the minimum buy-in plays.

INTERPRETATION NOTE

Arthur, who is seated in Seat 4, is playing $20–$40 hold'em and has only $150 in chips in front of him. He calls for a chip attendant, gives her ten one-hundred dollars bills, and tells the dealer that he is ". . . playing $1,000 behind." The dealer verifies this with the chip attendant, then announces to the table, "Seat four is playing $1,000 behind." With the chips in front of him added to those in transit, Arthur has $1,150 at his disposal.

2.45 MINIMUM CHIP REQUIREMENTS WHEN CHANGING TABLES

A player who changes tables does not have to purchase additional chips, so long as he transfers to another game of the same type at the same limits. A player transferring from one game to the same game at different limits, or from different games at the same limits, must purchase the minimum number of chips required for the new game.

INTERPRETATION NOTE

Transferring from one $15–$30 hold'em game to another $15–$30 hold'em game does not require a purchase of chips. This is considered a "table change," not a change of games.

A player moving from a $4–$8 hold'em game to a $6–$12 hold'em game is required to enter the new game with the required minimum buy-in. A player moving from $2–$4 Omaha/8 to $2–$4 Texas hold'em must enter the new game with the required minimum buy-in. Both of these moves are "game changes," not "table changes."

2.46 REQUIRED CHIP DENOMINATIONS

Games are played with chips of a specified denomination, and players are required to have at least the minimum required number of chips in that denomination.

INTERPRETATION NOTE

Too many large- or small-denomination chips are cumbersome and slow the pace of play. In a $2–$4 game, the appropriate denomination is $1 chips, in a $10–$20 or $20–$40 game the $5 chips work best; in a $50–$100 or $75–$150 game $25 chips are preferred. *Coloring up* (changing to chips larger than the preferred denomination) should be permitted only if a player has an excessive number of chips in front of her.

2.47 PLAYING LIGHT IN HOME GAMES

Home games are often played without table-stakes principles, and players in these games are permitted to *play light*, providing they make up their shortages before the start of the next hand.

INTERPRETATION NOTE

If you're running a home game, or playing in one, the rule regarding table stakes is an important one. Be sure to have this rule clarified by your host before play begins, because it can affect your betting strategy during the play of a hand. Although your authors favor table stakes for all games, we recognize that home games are often played without this requirement.

2.48 TRANSFERRING CHIPS FROM ONE PLAYER TO ANOTHER

If no player objects, chips may be transferred from one player to another in cash games. Chip transfers are never permitted in tournaments, and players caught transferring chips will be expelled from the tournament by the tournament director.

ALTERNATE RULE: Chip transfers are only permitted in fixed-limit games. Objections by other players to chip transfers must be made before shuffling begins for a new hand.

2.49 GOING ALL-IN AND COMPLETING BETS

A player with fewer chips than required to match or make a bet may put the remainder of his chips into the pot, in order to bet, or raise, or to call a bet or raise. This is referred to as *going all-in*. A player who is all-in is competing only for the portion of the pot to which he has contributed. A player who goes all-in should announce that to the dealer. Failure to announce an all-in status may, at the floor supervisor's discretion, result in the player being declared ineligible to win the pot.

An all-in wager of less than one-half a bet in fixed-limit games is not considered a *full bet*. If a player goes all-in by betting or raising less than half the required wager, players acting subsequently may fold or complete the bet by increasing it to a full wager.

An all-in wager of half a bet or more is considered a full bet, and a player responding to that wager may fold, call, or make a full raise. If the amount of the all-in bet or

INTERPRETATION NOTE

You're playing $15–$30 limit hold'em, the bet on the flop is $15, and Tom goes all-in for his last $5. Players who haven't yet acted may fold, call the $5 wager, or complete the bet to $15. They are not permitted to raise. Players who checked prior to Tom's all-in bet may only call Tom's wager; they may not complete the bet.

If Tom goes all-in for $5, and Mary completes the bet to $15, then anyone acting after Mary has the full range of options and may fold, call Mary's raise, or re-raise.

Completing an all-in wager that is less than half the normal bet is not considered a raise when determining how many raises may be made before reaching the limit. Instead, it is known as "action only."

This is the source of many arguments at the poker table, and yet it is more confusing than it is complex. If the wager is less than half the required bet, those yet to act may call that short bet or complete it to the full amount of the bet. Any player who checked before the all-in player's short bet may only call his short wager; they may not complete the bet. If one player completes the short bet, then subsequent players have the full range of wagering actions open to them and may fold, call, or raise.

raise is one-half the amount of the bet or more, then a player responding to that wager has the option of folding, calling the all-in action, or calling and raising one complete bet.

INTERPRETATION NOTE

For example, if a player makes an all-in $10 flop bet in a $20–$40 game, subsequent players may fold, call the $10 all-in bet, or raise an additional $20, for a total of $30.

ALTERNATE RULE: A player responding to such an all-in bet shall have the option of folding, calling the bet, or calling and raising by completing the bet and raising an additional bet. In a $20–$40 game played according to this alternate rule, a player raising a $10 all-in bet on the flop does so by completing the bet to $20 and then raising it to $40. A player raising a $20 all-in bet on the turn would complete the bet and raise it a full bet, for a total of $80.

2.50 INSURANCE

Insurance is prohibited in limit games but permitted in pot-limit and no-limit games. Since insurance is a private arrangement, management neither provides nor ensures the availability or opportunity to negotiate and purchase insurance. Management cannot enforce insurance arrangements among players. Any person who negotiates insurance during a hand and refuses to honor it shall be subject to discipline at the floor supervisor's discretion.

Similarly, in no-limit and pot-limit community-card

games, sometimes when there are two players left and one is all-in, the players agree to turn up their hands and, as insurance against a bad beat, run the turn and the river or just the river three times, awarding one-third, two-thirds, or the whole pot to each player with each alternate board.

INTERPRETATION NOTE

Insurance is a side bet between two players, or between one player and an outsider, usually called an *insurance man*, against a particular hand losing. Insurance is usually suggested before the final card is dealt. If the player who has taken insurance loses the pot, the person with whom she made this arrangement pays her some amount, usually equal to the value of the pot; if she wins, she pays that person some amount that is usually based on the odds against her losing.

2.51 (NO) SIDE BETS

Side bets during a game violate the table-stakes rules and are prohibited.

CHAPTER 3

PLAYER CONDUCT, ETIQUETTE, AND INTEGRITY

Poker has its own etiquette, and it's something that everyone learns when they begin to play regularly. Each of us behaves differently depending upon the circumstances in which we find ourselves, which is okay in general—we've been conditioned that way. But in poker, a set of standards has evolved, and this chapter will help you identify behavior that would be considered gauche, outré, and boorish in a poker setting, if not flatly illegal or unacceptable to the game.

Context is everything. You're expected to scream your head off at a horse race or boxing match, but maintain complete silence while you're standing by the eighteenth green, watching a top-notch golfer putt for a championship. The difference between the two defines etiquette, the unwritten code of conduct governing behavior in certain situations. Poker, like boxing, horse racing, going to church, and how you behave when visiting your in-laws, has an unwritten (until now) set of rules all its own.

Most of poker's protocol exists for good reason: it

speeds things along and keeps the game orderly. These unwritten rules are part and parcel of the game—just like the cards and chips. Indeed, for casino newcomers, poker's protocol and etiquette may take more getting used to than the actual game itself. Although violating a point of poker etiquette is not as serious as cheating, nor grounds for immediate banishment—as would be the case if you had physically threatened another player or an employee—these points of etiquette are necessary to maintain a well-run game.

3.1 UNACCEPTABLE CONDUCT

In order to provide a safe and comfortable place to play poker, management may expel players or visitors who are disruptive to the smooth functioning of fair poker games. The following actions are all incompatible with a smoothly running poker game and safe environment for players and employees alike. They are grounds for immediate expulsion:

- ✓ Carrying a weapon
- ✓ Making verbal or physical threats to any customer, guest, or employee
- ✓ Destroying or defacing property
- ✓ Throwing cards or other items at an employee or patron
- ✓ Cheating, or any form of collusion among players that violates the spirit of the "one player per hand" rule
- ✓ Using profanity or obscene language
- ✓ Creating a disturbance

✓ Conducting any form of illegal or unsanctioned gambling on the premises
✓ Persistent and intentional violations of poker etiquette

It's important to bear in mind that this list of expulsion-meriting activities is not meant to be comprehensive. It is illustrative only, and management may expel any player on an at-will basis.

While violating the precepts below don't rise to the level of cheating, threatening others, or carrying a weapon, and aren't likely to get you tossed from the premises, they do exemplify poker etiquette, and are all designed to ensure a smooth, quick, and fair game.

3.2 ACTING IN TURN

Each player is expected to act in turn as play proceeds in clockwise fashion around the table. This protects a player from providing too much information to opponents. In a no-limit cash game or tournament, it is important to wait until the amount of the bet or raise has been established before the next player acts. Folding before the amount of the raise has been established shall be deemed "acting out of turn," and if it happens repeatedly in a tournament, a penalty may be invoked.

3.3 ACTING IN A TIMELY MANNER

Players are expected to act promptly, although each player is entitled to a reasonable time to make a decision. A player wishing to take extra time before acting is expected to call

INTERPRETATION NOTE

If John bets and you plan to fold your hand, wait your turn before doing so. If you act out of turn, your opponent won't have to ponder your course of action before making her decision. If you're playing online this won't ever happen, since the software doesn't allow you to act out of turn.

"time" in order to stop the action. Failing to stop the action in this manner may cause the player to lose his right to act. See also Rule 3.21.

3.4 KEEPING CARDS IN PLAIN SIGHT

Keeping your cards on the table and in plain sight of the dealer, your opponents, and in sight of eye-in-the-sky security cameras that monitor play helps maintain the integrity of the game.

INTERPRETATION NOTE

There's no need to take your cards off the table in order to look at your hand; in fact, most casinos frown upon the practice. The best way to protect your hand is to keep it on the table and look at the cards by shielding them with both hands while lifting a corner of each card to peek at it.

3.5 DISCUSSING HANDS IN PLAY

Discussing hands in play is *forbidden*. During World War II the Allies used to say, "Loose lips sink ships," and that's advice you can take to heart at the poker table. Don't discuss your hand with neighbors at the table, even after you have folded. Although you are no longer contesting that particular pot, talking about the hand you folded violates the *one player per hand rule* and can yield information, particularly about cards that may no longer be in play. Loose talk can easily provide one of the remaining contestants with an edge. Even grimaces or groans at the appearance of face-up cards fall into this category. Something on the board elicited that reaction, so there's a high chance that the groaner's cards are closely connected to what the community cards or a player's up-cards display, and can be accounted for in that manner.

Taking it a step further, if you're playing online and sending instant messages to a buddy who's also in the game, or sharing via telephone or other technologies, you're not just stepping outside the bounds of etiquette, you're *cheating*, plain and simple.

3.6 GIVING LESSONS/ADVICE AT THE TABLE

Giving lessons or advice at the table is expressly forbidden and is grounds for immediate expulsion from the game, excepting certain "learners' games" where special, pre-announced rules may apply. Remember, one of poker's prime directives is this: *One player per hand*. Don't give an active player advice during the play of a hand, and don't advise him after the hand's conclusion, either. You'll either anger that player or others at the table.

INTERPRETATION NOTE

Although it may be easier to chat about hands online, the sophisticated game software and hand histories stored in host servers make it much easier for online casinos to spot any hanky-panky that may be going on.

Online casinos use very sophisticated software to monitor play, and whenever something doesn't look quite right, they are quick to analyze the facts at hand. Even consistent soft-play between two opponents will show up in the analysis of a large number of hands.

3.7 LOOKING AT OTHER PLAYERS' HANDS

She won't like it. I won't like it, and neither will anyone else at the table. Although they get fewer and fewer with each passing day, some things are still private in this world and poker hands are among them.

3.8 COLLUSION

Collusion comprises a variety of acts, but the net effect is the same: Collusion is a form of cheating that reduces the competitive elements of poker among participants. *Collusion always violates the Prime Directive of one player per hand.* To avoid collusive behavior or even the impression of collusion, each player is required to act only in his or her self-interest.

Collusion involves any intentional action taken by a player for the direct or indirect benefit of an opponent. Examples of collusion are listed below, although this list is illustrative only and is not intended to be all-inclusive. Collusive behavior may cause a player to forfeit his or her interest in the pot, face ejection from the game, be barred from the casino for some period of time, or be turned over to the local law enforcement agency. Examples are:

- ✓ Providing advice or assistance about how to play a hand, or how to bet or respond to a wager, or stating an opinion regarding a player's hand, or making a suggestion about the cards he might be holding in his hand when he bets or responds to action from another player
- ✓ Cheating by signaling information to a collusive partner in the game, or by using a specific device, card manipulation, or other deceptive tactics to gain an unfair advantage over opponents
- ✓ Introducing rigged, marked, daubed, or otherwise unfair decks into the game
- ✓ Providing information, or commenting about a hand or a suggested play to a player in the pot, or doing so loudly enough so that it may be overheard by other players at the table
- ✓ Soft-play agreements that result in refraining from betting at another player when head's-up or refunding money won to another player
- ✓ Agreeing to check down a hand with an opponent when a third player is all-in
- ✓ Telling another player to turn his hand face-up at the showdown

INTERPRETATION NOTE

The easiest way to avoid running afoul of collusive behavior is to refrain from making any statements or comments while a hand is in play.

3.9 DELIBERATE EXPOSURE OF CARDS

Intentionally exposing a card to induce or inhibit action is a serious breach of poker ethics, and in certain instances can be considered a form of collusion. It is never permitted.

3.10 CHIP MOVES AND MISLEADING GESTURES

Intentional "chip moves" designed to either encourage or discourage action are unethical. So is any form of misdirection or move aimed at inducing a player to act out of turn or to discover an opponent's intentions on subsequent betting decisions. Chip moves are contrary to poker's spirit and traditions. Reaching toward your chips as if you're going to bet is not a chip movement.

Players that persist in making chip moves are subject to discretionary punishment by a floor supervisor that may include banishment from the premises.

3.11 HAND MOTIONS DENOTE ACTION

Hand motions are considered to be a valid signal of action by a player and will be relied upon by the dealer and other players. Tapping the table or your arm or knee or anything or pointing to the table or just pointing in a downward direction is a check. Putting any part of your hand down on the table when it's your turn to act is a check. An upward hand motion, a thumbs-up signal, and other motions that may be construed by the dealer to indicate a raise commit a player to that action.

INTERPRETATION NOTE

Even ethical players sometimes get into trouble because they inadvertently tap their hands on the table while thinking. Players should be cognizant of the fact that an unconscious tapping on the table may well be deemed a check, thereby foreclosing an opportunity to bet.

3.12 INTEGRITY AND HONESTY

Trying to shortchange the pot or otherwise cheating is both forbidden and contrary to the spirit of the game. In a casino, cheating can get you barred or arrested; in a home game, the punishment might be much worse.

3.13 TABLE DEMEANOR

Patterns of culture vary from society to society, so what's acceptable table demeanor in one's home country might be considered boorish—if not downright rude—in another. Therefore, take your cues from the game you're playing in and act appropriately.

INTERPRETATION NOTE

We Americans can be a loud, unruly lot, given to insidious comments, caustic retorts, and snide remarks at the table, but as long as players are not providing information to others actively involved in a hand, "talking trash" is just part and parcel of the way we do things on the left side of the Atlantic. But some behavioral manifestations that are acceptable in Las Vegas, California, or Atlantic City would probably get you bounced from a UK poker room.

Conversation at a London poker table is sparse by American standards, and much more civilized. Likewise dress and bearing. Players dress better in the UK and on much of the European continent than they do in the States. A jacket, dress shoes, and a collared shirt, and even suits and ties are common attire in London casinos, a far cry from the typical American attire of jeans, sweats, or shorts, along with a T-shirt or polo shirt, ball cap, and sneakers or sandals.

Attire and demeanor are part of the cultural norms of the country where you happen to play, and it pays to know them beforehand. If you show up in London dressed like most players do when they play poker in California, Vegas, or Atlantic City, you probably won't even make it through the front door. It's not really that taxing to tune into the cultural norms of wherever you might find yourself, and good etiquette is nothing more than a means to a smooth, well-paced game.

3.14 CHIPS DENOTE ACTION

Chips always denote action, and chips placed in the pot demonstrate the intent of the player placing them, unless that player has made a different statement about his intentions prior to taking action. A player who puts fewer chips in the pot than necessary to call a bet must complete the call.

3.15 OVERSIZED CHIPS

Unless making a clear and unequivocal statement to the contrary, any player who puts more chips in the pot than required to call a bet is deemed to have called if the amount is less than a bet and a half. If it is more than a bet and a half, it will be considered a raise. The player may then complete the raise, or fold and relinquish the chips already committed to the pot.

INTERPRETATION NOTE

If a player is not aware that a pot has been raised, but places enough chips in the pot to call an unraised bet only, the dealer should advise him that the pot has been raised. The player can reconsider and change his action only if no one has acted after him.

If someone has acted behind him, the player who was unaware that the pot had been raised may choose to fold and forfeit any chips already committed to the pot or he may call the raise.

3.16 BETTING CIRCLES

Many poker tables have a betting circle—also called a *betting line, action line,* or *courtesy line*—that separates the inner region of the table from the outermost nine or ten inches nearest to the players. Each player's hole cards and chips should always remain in the region outside the betting circle during the course of play. In making a bet, any chips placed beyond the betting circle (or held in the air over that circle) are considered to have been wagered.

In the absence of a betting circle, the table area beyond the player's cards shall be deemed the betting circle. Chips placed on the table past a player's cards are to remain in the pot, even if the player is just counting chips to consider a call. A forward motion with chips in hand beyond the cards or into the betting circle is generally taken to represent a bet or a call. In many casinos, that forward motion means the movement of a hand with chips in it *beyond* the point where the player's hole cards are placed on the table. In other casinos what constitutes a *forward motion* is a judgment call.

Because both of these determining factors are not nearly as clear as moving chips beyond a betting circle, we recommend the use of betting circles in all poker games.

3.17 SPLASHING THE POT

Players should refrain from splashing the pot, best described as the energetic flinging or tossing of their chips toward the center of the table. Instead, each player's chips should be placed in front of the player as the bet, call, or raise is made, and stacked so the dealer can easily verify that the amount of money entering the pot is correct. When using

INTERPRETATION NOTE

Players often bring their hands forward with chips in them to rap the table as a declaration of checking, not betting. Dealers should caution players that bringing chips too far forward—and over the betting line, if one is present at the table—is considered a bet if another player acts. Merely reaching toward one's own chips and even lifting them straight above the chip stack shall not be deemed a bet.

chips of different denominations, players should place the highest-value chips on the bottom, lower denominations on top.

3.18 VERBAL AND PHYSICAL DECLARATIONS OF ACTION

Verbal declarations of action are always binding when made by a player *acting in turn*. A player acting out of turn will also be held to his or her verbal declarations unless intervening bets or raises change the action faced by the out-of-turn player. A player's first action is his binding action, whether it be a verbal declaration, a commitment of chips toward the pot, or a commonly accepted hand signal for checking or raising.

INTERPRETATION NOTE

Any player acting out of turn may not change that action when it is his or her turn to act. However, if David calls out of turn only to see that Abby—who is positioned to David's right—raises, then David may act on his hand when it's his turn.

However, David may not raise in this example; he may only call or fold, since a later attempt by him to raise could be construed as an attempt to mislead Abby about his betting intent.

3.19 PLACING CHIPS IN POT/STRING RAISES

Chips should be placed in the pot in a single motion.

3.20 CHECK-AND-RAISE

Players may check-and-raise in all permitted games, except certain forms of lowball. If the casino decides to offer a game where check-and-raise is prohibited, such as a beginner's game, a sign should be posted on the table and the dealer should inform all new players that check-raising is not permitted in this game.

3.21 CLOCKING OPPONENTS

When a player is slow to act, any other player may request that the dealer *clock* him. The dealer then gives that player one minute and ten seconds to act. After the first minute,

INTERPRETATION NOTE

Returning to your stack for additional chips is called a "string raise" and is expressly prohibited. A player may protect his or her right to raise by stating "Raise," followed by placing the proper amount of chips in the pot, and/or stating the amount of the raise. An oversized chip [see Rule 3.15] placed in the pot without declaring "raise" is a call, and the difference will be returned to the player.

If a player is uncertain about who raised, he may ask and expect to be answered by the dealer only until the dealer pulls in the pot, after which time the question may not be answered by the dealer or any player at the table.

the dealer counts down the remaining ten seconds. If the player hasn't acted at the conclusion of the count, his hand is declared dead if he is facing action, or he is deemed to have checked if he is not responding to another player's action.

3.22 CALLING ATTENTION TO PROCEDURAL ERRORS

Whenever a player becomes aware of a procedural error, or notices that the action has passed his position in error and he has not had time to act, he can protect his rights by immediately calling "time" to stop the action, then voice his objection. If a player waits until there has been action by

INTERPRETATION NOTE

If Joe is slow to act, you can request the dealer to "put a clock on him." This procedure will result in a one-minute period of time, followed by a dealer countdown from ten to one. At the end of that count, if the player has not acted on his hand, it is considered a check if the player was not facing an opponent's bet, or a folded hand that is now dead if the player failed to respond to another player's action.

two players, or by a player and the dealer, the error will be corrected only if a fouled deck is involved.

3.22.1 CALLING SHORT AND WITHDRAWING BETS

In a cash game, when a player's call does not include a raised amount or kill, the player must leave the money she has wagered in the pot and has the option of folding her cards or making the wager correct.

ALTERNATE RULE: In a cash game, when a player's call does not include a raised amount or kill, the player will be allowed to withdraw his bet if no action, or no *significant* action, has occurred after him. If action has occurred, he must either forfeit the amount he has already placed in the pot and fold his cards or add chips to make his wager the correct amount.

3.23 DISCARDING HANDS

A player who throws his cards face down with a forward motion surrenders his hand along with his interest in the pot. His hand is considered dead if it is commingled with the muck or another player has acted after him. If the hand is retrievable, the floor supervisor may rule that it is "live"—provided this is in the best interests of the game.

INTERPRETATION NOTE

Hands are considered dead if any of the following events transpire:

✓ The cards touch the muck
✓ The cards are tossed into an opponent's cards either face up or face down
✓ If a player passes and another player then acts
✓ If the hand does not contain the correct number of cards
✓ If a player turns his up-cards face down or mixes his up-cards and down-cards in a stud game
✓ If a player verbally relinquishes her interest in the pot by stating "I fold," or "You win"

3.24 CHECKING DOWN HANDS

Explicitly agreeing to check a hand to conclusion when a third player is all-in is a form of collusion and a breach of etiquette.

INTERPRETATION NOTE

This point of etiquette is predicated on agreeing to check a hand to conclusion. There's no breach of etiquette if both players independently decide to check the hand to its conclusion with a third player all-in as long as there is no explicit agreement to do so.

3.25 ASSISTING OTHER PLAYERS

Reading a hand for another player before it has been placed face up at the showdown violates the spirit of the "one player per hand" rule. Asking or directing a player to turn a hand face up at the showdown violates the spirit of the "one player per hand" rule.

3.26 FOLDING TOWARD THE MUCK

When folding, cards should be directed to the muck.

3.27 CARDS PITCHED OFF TABLE

This is a violation of poker etiquette and if deemed by a floor supervisor to be deliberate, it may result in time away from the table.

3.28 TOKING

Tipping the dealer—it's called "toking" in poker parlance—is customary when you win a pot. If you're unsure of how much to toke, just take your cues from the others at the table. There's no toking online, which is one of the niceties about playing on the Internet.

3.29 MOBILE PHONES

Using a cell phone at the table is a violation of etiquette. To make or receive a call, please step away from the table. Players using a cell phone will be dealt out of the hand they are in.

3.30 ITEMS ON TABLE

The only items permissible on the table are chips, cash and, if the game allows, one foreign chip or card cap, and drink holder and drink.

3.31 SMOKING

No smoking is permitted in the card room, other than in designated areas with separate ventilation systems.

INTERPERETATION NOTE

The authors agree with Jan Fisher that smoking should also be forbidden in front of the card room. Non-smoking players should not have to walk through "the gauntlet of smoke" to get to the no-smoking poker area.

3.32 WINNING AND LOSING WELL

Not a rule, per se, but our guidance toward improving the overall quality of your game. Don't gloat. Don't make fun of other players; and don't whine, complain, blame the dealer, cards, or other players when you lose. You won't be the first player to lose to an impossible draw against long odds. *Bad beats* happen to everyone and no one really wants to hear about it.

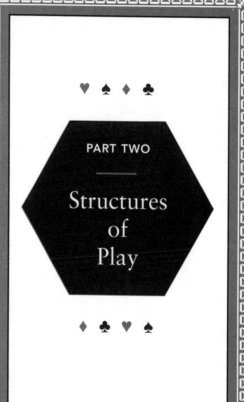

♥ ♠ ♦ ♣

PART TWO

Structures
of
Play

♦ ♣ ♥ ♠

CHAPTER 4

THE DECK AND CARDS

4.1 DECK COMPOSITION

Poker is played with a fifty-two-card deck comprising four suits—clubs, diamonds, hearts, and spades—with thirteen ranks each: deuce, 3, 4, 5, 6, 7, 8, 9, 10, jack, queen, king, ace.

Draw and lowball are played with a joker—it's also called a "bug"—added to the deck. It's not strictly a wild card, because it does not stand for *any* card you need to complete your hand. In draw, the joker is used as an ace, or to complete straights or flushes. In lowball, it is the lowest card not in a player's hand.

Except for the use of a bug in draw and lowball games, wild cards are never used in casinos, although they are common in home games.

Suits have no bearing on the ranking of hands, but can be used in determining the lowest or highest card for a forced bet.

INTERPRETATION NOTE

While a flush of one suit does not take priority over another suit if the ranks of the cards are identical, the deuce of clubs will make a forced bet in any game in which the lowest card is required to make a token bet, or "bring-in." In that case, the lowest suit is clubs, followed by diamonds, hearts, and spades. It's the alphabet, from lowest suit to highest, if you need a memory aid.

4.2 HANDS BEGIN WITH SHUFFLE

Each hand begins with a shuffle. Once the shuffle begins, the hand is in play. Play proceeds clockwise with each player acting after the player to her immediate right.

4.3 BRING-IN BETS

In stud games the lowest up-card (or the highest up-card in eight-or-better or in razz) is required to make an initial forced bet, called the *bring-in*. It is usually equivalent to one-third or one-half a small bet in fixed-limit games.

4.4 BLIND BETS

In hold'em games the first two players after the dealer button are required to post a blind bet before they are dealt any cards. The small blind is a portion of a small bet, typically one-third to two-thirds of the small bet. The second player posts a big blind, equivalent to a full small bet.

Players must respond in turn to these forced bets by folding, calling, or raising. Action proceeds clockwise, and once play begins, the hand continues until the pot is awarded.

4.5 NUMBER OF BETTING ROUNDS

The number of betting rounds varies by game. Draw games have two betting rounds, one before the draw and one after.

Flop games, including Texas hold'em and Omaha/8, have four betting rounds. The first round occurs before the flop and is followed by three subsequent betting rounds—the first of these occurs after the "flop," the first three community cards—is dealt; the second, after the "turn" or fourth community card; and the third (and fourth overall, including the pre-flop betting) after the "river," which is the fifth and last community card.

Stud games have five betting rounds. One occurs after the first three cards have been dealt, and one after each subsequent card.

4.6 NUMBER OF PLAYERS PER GAME

A poker game typically has two to ten players. While more are possible—you can play hold'em with twenty-two players—anything above ten is unwieldy and impractical.

In seven-card stud games the maximum number of players is eight.

Draw and lowball games are usually played eight-handed.

4.7 WINNING A POT

Hands are won in either of two ways: you show down the best hand at the conclusion of all the betting rounds or you win because all of your opponents have folded their hands. In this case, you may have had the best hand or you may have been bluffing—it doesn't matter—because once your opponents have surrendered their claim to the pot, it's yours.

In games like seven-card stud and Texas hold'em the best hand is a high hand. In other games, like lowball and razz, the best hand is a low hand. In split-pot games, like seven-card stud, high-low split, eight-or-better (seven-stud/8) and Omaha high-low split, eight-or-better (Omaha/8) the best high hand and the best low hand (providing someone makes a low hand comprised of five unpaired cards with a rank of eight or lower) split the pot. While a high hand will always be made, there won't necessarily be a low hand. And when there's no low hand, the high hand wins the entire pot.

Each poker hand begins as a chase for the blinds or the antes. If antes are used, each player must post this token amount of money in order to receive cards. If blinds are employed, one or two players are required to post a bet or portion of a bet (these are the "blinds") before the hand is dealt. This requirement rotates around the table so that each player pays her fair share.

Each time a round of cards is dealt, players have an opportunity to check, bet, fold, call, or raise. Any time a player decides to fold, or forfeit his interest in the pot, he may release his hand when it is his turn to act. When a player folds a hand, he is not required to place any more money in the pot. If you bet or raise and no one calls, the pot belongs to you, at which time the cards are gathered and shuffled and the next hand is dealt. If there are two or more players still active at the end of the hand, the best hand wins the pot.

While there are different rules for each specific version, poker really is this simple. Yet within its simplicity lies a wonderfully textured game structure that is always fascinating, always enjoyable, and for some a lifelong source of pleasure.

4.8 HAND RANKINGS

Seven-card stud and Texas hold'em are the two most popular forms of poker in which the high hand wins at a showdown. These games are played with a fifty-two-card deck—no jokers—comprising four suits: spades, hearts, diamonds, and clubs. Each suit is equal in value, and there are thirteen cards of each suit. The ace is the highest-ranking card in a suit, followed by king, queen, jack, and ten through deuce, in descending order. An ace may also be used as the lowest ranking card in a five-high straight, which is also called a "wheel" or "bicycle."

Although stud and hold'em are played with seven cards, the best hand refers to the best five-card hand that can be made from those seven cards. Hand rankings are a function of probability. The rarer the hand, the more valuable it is.

4.8.1 STRAIGHT FLUSH

A straight flush is five cards of the same suit in sequence, such as 9♥ 8♥ 7♥ 6♥ 5♥. A royal flush is simply an ace-high straight flush, and is the best possible hand in poker.

INTERPRETATION NOTE

If you're playing draw, the best hand is five aces. Since the bug can be used as another ace, it is possible to hold five of them, and that's rarer than a straight flush. But don't be surprised if you play a lifetime without holding that hand.

4.8.2 FOUR-OF-A-KIND

Four-of-a-kind, or "quads," is a five-card hand that comprises all the cards of one rank, plus one unrelated card, such as J♥ J♠ J♦ J♣ 5♣. The higher the rank, the better the hand.

4.8.3 FULL HOUSE

Three cards of one rank and a pair of another make a full house. The rank of the full house is determined by the three-card grouping, not the pair; no competing full houses could contain the same three-card grouping. A hand like 9♥ 9♣ 9♦ 5♦ 5♣ is referred to as ". . . nines full of fives." If the hand contained three fives and two nines, it would be called "fives full of nines."

4.8.4 FLUSH

A flush is any five cards of the same suit. The cards are not in sequence. If they were, it would be a straight flush. If there is more than one flush, the winning hand is determined by the rank order of the highest card—or cards—in the flush. A flush consisting of A♥ Q♥ J♥ 6♥ 5♥, is higher than A♣ Q♣ J♣ 4♣ 3♣.

4.8.5 STRAIGHT

Five sequenced cards, not all of the same suit, comprise a straight. If more than one straight is present, then the highest card in the sequence determines the winning hand. This J♥ T♠ 9♦ 8♦ 7♣ jack-high straight will beat this 9♠ 8♠ 7♦ 6♠ 5♣ nine-high straight.

4.8.6 THREE-OF-A-KIND

Three cards of the same rank, along with two unrelated cards is called three-of-a-kind. It's also referred to as "trips," or a "set." If you held 8♣ 8♥ 8♠ K♦ 4♣ you could refer to it as ". . . trip eights," or "a set of eights."

4.8.7 TWO PAIR

Two cards of one rank along with two cards of another rank and one unrelated card comprises two pair. The higher of the two pairs determines the overall superiority of the hand. If two players hold two pair and each has the same high pair, then the rank of the second pair determines the winner. If both players hold the same two pair, then the rank of the unrelated side card (referred to as the "kicker") determines the winning hand, and if the hand is identical even through the kicker (suits don't count), then the players split the pot. In this example, Q♣ Q♥ 8♠ 8♦ 4♣ (queens and eights) is superior to Q♠ Q♦ 5♣ 5♠ K♦ (queens and fives).

4.8.8 ONE PAIR

One pair is simply two cards of one rank and three unrelated cards. If two players hold the same pair, then the value of the unrelated side cards (the kickers) determines the winning hand.

4.8.9 NO PAIR

Five unrelated cards. When no player has a pair, the winning hand is determined by the rank order of the unrelated cards. Suits do not matter unless all five cards are of the same suite, which would be a *flush*.

4.8.10 LOW HANDS

In split-pot games such as Omaha/8, the best low hand, comprised of five unrelated cards with the rank of eight or lower, captures half the pot. The relative strength of a low hand is based on its highest (worst) card, then its second-worst card, and so on. A hand like 7♣6♥4♠ 3♦A♣ will beat 7♦6♣5♥3♠A♦, but will lose to 7♠ 4♥3♥2♣A♠.

INTERPRETATION NOTE

Determining the best low hand takes a bit of practice, but if you always begin with the highest of the low cards and continue in descending order, you won't go wrong.

In determining the highest possible five-card hand, whenever all five cards are not used to make a hand, such as with three of a kind, two pair, or one pair, the rank of the side cards (the kickers) determines which hand is better. If the board were A-A-9-3-2 and Shannon's hole cards are A-10 while Heather's hole cards are A-6, Shannon will win the pot since the best overall five-card hand wins: Shannon has A-A-A-T-9, while Heather has A-A-A-9-6.

In split-pot and low-only games (not counting Kansas City *deuce-to-seven* lowball, which is detailed elsewhere), the following is the ranking of the best low hands:

5-4-3-2-A (called a "wheel")
6-4-3-2-A (smooth six)
6-5-3-2-A
6-5-4-2-A
6-5-4-3-A
6-5-4-3-2
7-4-3-2-A (smooth seven, perfect seven, seven A-B-C, or seven-slick)
7-5-3-2-A

This progression continues all the way through the smallest pair, trips, full houses, four of a kind, and straight flushes. Straights and flushes do not count against low hands, except when playing Kansas City lowball. Because aces play for high or low, a pair of aces is a better low hand than a pair of deuces.

Most high-low split games require an eight-or-better qualifier for low. If no player holds five unpaired cards with the rank of eight or lower, then no hand has *qualified*—the high hand scoops the entire pot.

Kansas City (deuce-to-seven) lowball, which is popular in tournaments but seldom spread as a cash game, employs different rules, and therefore has different rankings than the low hands shown above. In deuce-to-seven lowball, straights and flushes count against you, and an ace is only a high card, never a low one. Consequently, the best hand in Kansas City lowball is 7-5-4-3-2.

INTERPRETATION NOTE

Determining the best low hand often causes trouble for beginning players. To read a low hand, arrange them in descending order, from high to low. Remember that an ace is low, so that a 7-5-4-2-A is lower than 7-5-4-3-A. What can cause a problem is reading the ace as a high card, not the low needed for this purpose. Just place it where it belongs—all the way to the right, as the lowest card in the deck—and you should be able to read low hands perfectly.

4.9 SHUFFLING

All hands begin when the dealer assembles the cards for shuffling. Once this process is under way, the hand must be dealt. The only exceptions are a misdeal, which requires a new shuffle, or a countervailing decision from a floor supervisor.

Dealers are required to shuffle the cards at least three times and riffle them once. The usual pattern is shuffle, shuffle, riffle, shuffle, followed by a cut. Dealers should begin and end with a shuffle, then cut the cards using one hand.

4.10 MECHANICAL SHUFFLING MACHINES

When a mechanical shuffling device is employed, the hand officially begins when the shuffled deck leaves the dealer's

hand as he places it on the table to be cut. The hand officially ends when the dealer releases the used deck to the
shuffling machine.

INTERPRETATION NOTE

Mechanical shuffling machines are growing in popularity. They allow for more hands to be dealt per
hour, because one deck is automatically shuffled
while another deck is in use for the hand in play.
These devices are generally built into a table and
set to the right of the dealer, about parallel to where
the flop is spread. Shufflers generally have two com-
partments; one for the newly shuffled deck and the
other to receive the used deck that will be shuffled
while the forthcoming hand is in play.

After removing the newly shuffled deck from the
shuffling machine, the dealer should place the deck
on the table and release his hand from the deck.
Then he should cut the deck onto his cut-card and
deal the hand. At the hand's end, the dealer should
scramble the cards slightly as he brings the old deck
together, and then place the used deck into the
shuffling machine using one hand.

Whenever the shuffling machine malfunctions,
which is to say the red light comes on, the floor
supervisor, and not the dealer, should reach into the
machine and clear it. If the machine continues to
malfunction, the dealer shall continue to shuffle and
deal manually.

4.11 DEALER RESPONSIBILITIES

A dealer is responsible for maintaining the game's pace and accuracy. He is accountable for ensuring that all blinds or antes are properly posted and for prompting players when they are required to take action.

A dealer should announce the number of active players in each hand and make sure the pot is correct. Dealers should pull all bets into the pot only when each betting round is complete. Until that time, all bets and blinds are to remain in front of players. In high-low split games such as seven-stud/8 and Omaha/8, when only two players are actively contesting the pot, the dealer should leave the bets in front of each player until the pot is awarded.

A dead blind is an exception to this procedure. It should be moved to the center of the pot after the cards have been cut, but before they have been dealt, in order to prevent confusion among other players as to whether the dead blind is a wager from one of his or her opponents.

Players are never permitted to make change from the pot or from touching other players' bets or chips.

Before dealing, the dealer should tap the table as a signal that he is about to burn a card and deal. This signal allows players to alert the dealer if the betting is incomplete or there is some other irregularity that should be rectified before dealing the cards.

When all dealing is complete, the dealer should drop the deck with the cards spread out, rather than stacked. After the showdown or end of the hand, the dealer commingles the discards with the deck stub, to prevent untoward *rabbit hunting*. He should not place the discards on the top or bottom of the deck stub. The dealer then pushes the pot to the winner before moving the button.

In games where the deck is hand-shuffled by the dealer instead of by a shuffling machine, the *soft scramble* is the last act of the old hand; the initial shuffle constitutes the beginning of a new hand.

4.12 BURN-CARD PLACEMENT

Burn cards should be placed under the edge of the pot without being flashed to the players.

4.13 CARDS DEALT OFF TABLE

Any card dealt off the table or even suspected to have been exposed is considered to be an exposed card. If a player's card is flashed, that card is to be exposed to all players and announced by the dealer.

A card exposed by a player will not be replaced. But a card pitched by the dealer that strikes a player's hand and is exposed will be replaced. The exposed card will be displayed to the table and announced by the dealer.

4.14 BOXED CARDS

A card facing the wrong way in the deck is called a *boxed card*. When a card is boxed, the next card in the deck is dealt to the player, just as if the boxed card didn't exist. If two or more boxed cards are discovered early in a hand, the deck is considered a *fouled deck* and the hand becomes a misdeal. But if the second and subsequent boxed cards are found only after substantial action has taken place, the play of the hand continues just as if only one boxed card were discovered.

4.15 FOULED DECK

A deck can be fouled for any of the following reasons:

- ✓ The deck contains more or less than the correct amount of cards.
- ✓ The deck contains two or more boxed cards and no substantial action has occurred.
- ✓ The deck contains duplicate cards.
- ✓ The deck contains non-standard cards such as a joker.
- ✓ The deck contains cards with a different-colored back.

When the deck is fouled, betting ceases and any money in the pot is returned to the players. It is treated as though the fouled hand never took place, and the next hand is played with the button and blinds in the same positions.

If the community cards are dealt before the action is complete, the correct procedure involves returning the flop cards to the deck, but leaving the burn card in place. Once the action has been completed, the flop cards will be reshuffled into the deck. The flop will then be dealt once again, using the original burn card.

An improperly dealt turn card will be set aside. The dealer will then burn and turn again. This allows the card that would have been dealt on the river to become the turn card. When betting on the turn concludes, the dealer should shuffle the incorrectly dealt turn card into the deck, then deal a river card without burning. The turn's original burn card is not included in the shuffle.

If the river is dealt incorrectly, the dealer will shuffle the improperly dealt card back into the deck, and then deal a new river card without burning.

4.16 MARKED OR MARRED CARDS

If a card is marked or marred in any way, the dealer is required to change decks and call for a setup. A new deck will be spread face up to determine that it is correctly composed. New decks should be scrambled face up and then face down. A new deck should be shuffled five times.

Although players are always free to request a deck change, decks will not be changed until a deck has been in play for at least one orbit of the table [see Rule 2.6]. Players may request a setup no more frequently than once per hour, except for a marred card or improperly composed deck.

ALTERNATE RULE: Setups shall not be made more than once per half hour.

4.17 MISDEALS

Misdeals occur for a wide variety of reasons: failing to shuffle or cut, dealing too many cards, dealing to the wrong player first, dealing out a player who should be in the hand, exposing the first or second card dealt, finding two or more boxed cards, or dealing a hand to a player who hasn't posted a blind or ante. That's only a partial list. During the initial round of dealing, a misdeal automatically results in a new deal, unless two or more players acted. If two or more players have acted ("significant action"), the hand continues.

In games using communal cards, if the dealer inadvertently exposes a card that she is dealing to a player, that card becomes the "burn" card, and the card that would have been the burn card goes to the player. If the dealer exposes two cards, it is a misdeal. In the case of other dealer errors that result in a change to the cards a player would have received, the floor supervisor must be called for a decision. If a dealer error does not affect the cards a player would receive, or give an advantage to any other player, the dealer may correct the error without a floor supervi-

INTERPRETATION NOTE

The goal here is to reconstitute the improperly dropped deck as closely as possible to the way it would have been had the dealer not dropped the deck prematurely, thereby preserving the integrity of the board. That means discards are excluded, as are burn cards, as those cards (exposed or not) are known to not be part of the remaining deck.

If there's any doubt as to whether a card is a discard or not, it's better to exclude it from the reconstituted deck than include it. After all, if the reconstituted deck represents random cards that have not already been played, it is fair to all concerned.

sor's presence, unless a player objects. Whenever there is doubt, dealers are required to call a floor supervisor to make a decision.

When the deck is dropped to the table, the dealer should pick up and continue to use the improperly dropped deck as long as the top of the deck can be determined. If there is any debate as to the top of the deck, or any other doubts (such as accidental exposure of cards), a floor supervisor is to be called. Under these circumstances, the dealer should reshuffle the unused cards and cut them. Discards and burn cards are not included in the reconstituted deck. The dealer will take the reconstituted deck, then burn and deal normally.

※※※※※※※※※※※

Tournament Director Jan Fisher relates this story.

TOPIC
Dealer Errors: The Case of the Irretrievably Mucked Deck

I get letters all of the time from players asking about a poor decision and what I would have done. Recently, I heard of a no-limit tournament hand in which a player raised all-in and was called, but the dealer didn't see the call. He irretrievably mucked the deck and pushed the pot. The player who called spoke up immediately. The floor split the pot!!! They asked me what I would have done.

Since the players still had their hole cards, I would have reshuffled the cards—ALL of them—minus any cards that might have been exposed and known to be out of play as they would have been in a player's hand. I would then have had a new flop, turn, and river. The players would have held the same cards for the showdown (since one player was all-in and the other had called, making no further decisions necessary). This seemed like a no-brainer to me, but they thought it was God-like. Go figure.

CHAPTER 5

BETTING STRUCTURES

5.1 FIXED-LIMIT POKER

Most of the poker games found in casinos in the United States are fixed-limit games. Fixed-limit poker is generally described by the game's betting limits, such as $4–$8 hold'em, $10–$20 Omaha/8, or $75–$150 seven-card stud.

5.1.1 BETTING STRUCTURES FOR COMMUNITY-CARD GAMES

Fixed-limit games typically have two betting limits, with the given betting limit usually doubling at a certain point in the game or otherwise going from the lower to the higher limit. In *board* games such as Texas hold'em and Omaha, where community cards are employed, there are a total of four betting rounds. The first two rounds of wagering—those that take place before and on the flop—are at the lower limit. During the last two wagering rounds—at the turn and on the river—bets are made at the higher limit.

5.1.2 BETTING STRUCTURES FOR STUD GAMES

In seven-card stud, fixed-limit betting is at the lower limit on third and fourth streets, with the wagering doubling for fifth, sixth, and seventh streets. In other words, for all stud games (including seven-card stud, seven-stud/8, and razz), the first two wagering rounds are at the lower limit while the last three are at the higher limit. The exception to this rule occurs in seven-card stud. Whenever an open pair (a face-up pair in two cards) shows on fourth street, any player has the option to bet at the higher limit. This rule does not apply in seven-stud/8, razz, or other split-pot or low-only stud poker games.

5.1.3 BETTING STRUCTURES FOR DRAW GAMES

In fixed-limit draw and lowball games that feature only two rounds of betting, wagers are made at the lower limit on the first round of betting, with wagering doubling on the second round of betting after cards have been exchanged.

While this procedure is true for all fixed-limit, high-draw games, it is not the rule for all draw lowball games. Some lowball games are played with both rounds of betting at the same limit.

5.2 NO-LIMIT POKER

Players may bet all the money that they have in play at any time, with the provision that money wagered must be in play before the hand begins. This is the basic concept of *table stakes.* While a player may put more money on the table or buy more chips only between hands, he is forbidden from removing money or chips from the table—other than a token amount for purchasing food or beverages, or tipping—unless he leaves the game.

This rule, which is sometimes called *stakes play,* applies in all public card rooms and to many private games, too.

INTERPRETATION NOTE

In fixed-limit games, you have limited options in deciding how much to wager. With the exception of choosing whether to bet either the smaller amount or to make a double bet on fourth street in a seven-card stud game when an open pair shows, your decision is only about whether you will bet or raise (or fold), never about the amount of the raise.

If the game is $4–$8 hold'em and Joyce bets $4 on the flop, Marv, who is next to act, has only three options to choose from: he can fold, call Joyce's $4 bet, or raise another $4, thus making it $8 "to go" for anyone who has not yet acted. If this was a no-limit game, Marv could fold, call, or raise any amount up to all the chips in front of him.

Other than adherence to the concept of table stakes, there are no limits on the amount a player may bet, nor is there any limit on the number of raises on any betting round.

5.2.1 RAISING REQUIREMENTS

With the exception of a player who goes all-in, bets must be sized at least equal to the bring-in designated for that game. Raises must be at least equal to the previous bet or raise on that round. The only exception is an all-in wager.

INTERPRETATION NOTE

As a practical matter, by the time the pot is raised and re-raised a few times, players are likely to be all-in. Therefore, except in the rare instances that two or more players try to bait each other through a series of small raises, the lack of a cap on the number of allowable raises is usually a moot point.

5.2.2 CHECK-RAISING ALL-IN BETS

A player who has checked may not raise an all-in bet that is less than the minimum bring-in. A player who checked and called may not raise an all-in bet that is less than the last bet or raise.

INTERPRETATION NOTE

If Ron bets $20 and Amber wishes to raise, she must do so by raising at least $20 more. However, if Amber only has, say, $30 total in chips, she can move all-in for that amount.

In this example, if Amber has at least $40 in chips, then she must commit at least $40 to the pot in order to re-raise Ron—in essence she is matching Ron's initial $20 bet, then raising at least that amount herself. Should she wish to re-raise by more than the minimum re-raise amount ($40), she can bet anything up to and including the sum total of chips in her possession.

INTERPRETATION NOTE

Let's assume that Manny bets $20, Moe raises another $20 (for a total bet of $40), and Jack re-raises all-in by committing his last $50 to the pot. In essence, Jack has called Manny's initial bet and Moe's raise, which made the bet $40 to go, then raised again with his final $10.

If Manny calls Jack's $10 all-in raise, Moe does not have an option to raise again, because he was raised by a player posting less than a full raise to the pot. However, Manny, whose initial bet was raised by Moe, has all options available to him. In this example, Manny may fold his hand, call the raises, or re-raise. If Manny elects to raise, then Moe will have all available options open to him because he is now reacting to Manny's full raise.

5.2.3 BET DECLARATIONS

A player announcing a bet or a raise of a given amount will be held to his verbal declaration in the event that he puts a different amount into the pot. If he does put a different amount into the pot, the player will be held to his verbal declaration.

5.2.4 OVERSIZED CHIPS, NO-LIMIT

When a player who is responding to a bet or raise places an oversized chip or bill into the pot and does so without comment or declaration, that chip or bill will be considered a call, not a raise. Pre-flop, when blinds are posted, a single oversized chip is deemed a call.

After the flop, if a player is not facing a bet or raise by another player and commits an oversized chip or bill to the pot, it will be presumed to be a wager for the entire amount of that bill or chip.

INTERPRETATION NOTE

Oversized chips and bills often result in arguments at the poker table because they frequently lead to uncertainty about a player's intention. To avoid arguments, to speed the game along, and to make your actions crystal clear, we advise stating the size of your bet or raise anytime an oversized bill or chip is committed to the pot.

Moreover, by announcing your raise, you are entitled to use more than one motion to place chips in the pot.

The following story was provided by Sheree Bykofsky.

TOPIC
Declaring All-In: The Case of the Not All-In

I watched several rules get tortured in the poker room of a well-known casino—and in this case, several at one time. The game was one-two no-limit. A

man made a bet for $40. The woman after him put $70 into the pot without saying all-in. She left a one-dollar chip on her card as a card-cover. The cards were not turned over because, as the dealer rightly said, she was not all-in (because she had made a single motion without declaring "all-in"). But her $70 bet was not double the $40 bet and therefore should have been deemed a call. The other player called the $30 difference and waited until the river to put her all-in for one dollar.

Assessment

The woman would have saved $30 on the turn if the dealer had refused to allow her raise to stand. She may have then realized that her pocket kings would not stand up with an ace on board.

※※※※※※※※※※※

5.2.5 ASKING FOR OPPONENTS' CHIP COUNTS

"How much does he have in front of him?" If you play pot- or no-limit, you'll hear this often. Any player has the right to know exactly how much money an opponent has in play. For that reason, players are required to provide an unimpeded view of their chips and cash to others at all times. Players are also required to stack their chips so that large denominations are in front, and therefore more readily visible, while smaller denominations are in the rear.

INTERPRETATION NOTE

Stacking larger chips in front and smaller chips in the rear, preferably in stacks of twenty chips each, makes it easier for players to estimate the amount of chips an opponent has in play without needlessly holding up play by asking that a player's stacks be counted down.

One word of caution: While it's within a player's right to ask for a countdown in order to accurately gauge the number of chips an opponent holds, repeatedly asking for countdowns is itself a breach of poker etiquette.

5.3 POT-LIMIT POKER

This is the predominant form of poker spread in the United Kingdom and many parts of Europe. It has gained in popularity online, and Omaha played for high only is usually played as a pot-limit game.

5.3.1 BETTING IN POT-LIMIT

Most pot-limit games use a structure based on blinds instead of antes. Under pot-limit rules, players may bet as little as the minimum bring-in or as much as the amount of the pot.

5.3.2 OPENING BETS IN POT-LIMIT

The opening bet for a player responding to the blind may be any amount between the big blind and a sum four times

INTERPRETATION NOTE

If the blinds are $5 and $10, a player may open by raising to $40. Here's how this is calculated:

The small $5 blind is treated as a complete bet of $10 for purposes of calculating the pot's size. This treatment creates an effective pot of $20, made up of two separate $10 wagers. If Nathan wants to make a pot-sized raise, he will first match the big blind's $10 wager, which brings the pot to a total of $30, then he will raise the size of the pot. Thus, he will be adding $40 to the pot.

His other options would have been to fold, to call for $10, or to raise any amount from $20 to $40 in five-dollar increments.

Players acting after Nathan also treat the $5 small blind as though it were a full $10 bet when calculating the size of the pot.

This procedure simplifies things dramatically, especially when the small blind uses a lower denomination chip than the big blind.

the size of the big blind. The bring-in bet can sometimes exceed the sum of the blinds and antes because of rounding.

For ease of play, the pot size is sometimes rounded upward. For instance, if the pot size was predicated on $25 chips, then a pot size of $90 would be treated as though it were $100.

In pot-limit hold'em and pot-limit Omaha cash games,

the small blind is treated as though it were the size of the big blind for computing the size of the pot.

EXCEPTION: Treating the small blind as if it were a big blind for purposes of calculating the pot size is not done in tournament play. In pot-limit tournaments, exact calculations are used, and a pot that is seeded with a $5 blind and a $10 blind will be treated as a $15 pot, not a pot of $20.

INTERPRETATION NOTE

If the blinds are $5 and $10 in a tournament, a player may open by raising to $35. The $5 and $10 blinds total $15. If Leonard wants to make a pot-sized raise, he will first match the big blind's $10 wager, which brings the pot to a total of $25, and then he will raise the size of the pot, an additional $25. Thus he will be adding $35 to the pot, and he will have raised a total of 3.5 times the big blind.

When playing online, the issues regarding an accurate count of the pot are nonexistent. The software does it instantaneously and accurately.

5.3.3 SIZING THE POT

The pot's size is always rounded upward to an even multiple of the minimum betting unit when determining the maximum allowable wager. Any odd chips that are smaller than the minimum betting unit will be combined and treated as though they were one complete minimum betting unit.

Any chips that have been raked or otherwise removed from the pot are treated as though they are still part of the pot.

The maximum permissible raise is calculated by first figuring the amount needed for the raiser to call the bet he is responding to, then matching the size of that bet, including the amount required to call. A player is eligible to raise the amount of the pot after he has called the bet he is facing.

INTERPRETATION NOTE

If the pot contains $50 and Jimmy bets the pot, then Mark can raise another $200. In essence, what he is doing is matching the pot-sized bet of $50, bringing the pot to a total of $150, then raising another $150. This now brings the total amount of money in the pot to $300.

If that sounds like he is raising himself, he is. But that's the nature of pot-limit betting structures.

5.3.4 OVERBETTING THE POT

If a player's bet exceeds the size of the pot, the excess will be returned to him. The dealer, and every player in the game, has an ethical obligation to point out any wager appearing to exceed the size of the pot. An oversized wager may be corrected at any time until all players have acted on it.

However, if more than two players have acted on the oversized wager, the floor supervisor has the option of ruling that all bets shall be predicated on the size of the *overbet* rather than the size of the pot.

5.3.5 OVERSIZED CHIPS, POT-LIMIT

Any chip or bill larger than the pot that is wagered without comment is considered a pot-sized bet, unless that wager is in response to another player's bet or raise. In that case, an oversized chip committed to the pot by a player facing action from an opponent is considered to be a call, not a raise.

INTERPRETATION NOTE

Betting an oversized chip without comment is considered to be a pot-sized wager. Responding without comment to an opponent's bet or raise with an oversized chip will be considered a call.

5.4 OTHER POT-LIMIT STRUCTURES

Pot-limit is also played with variations in the betting structure:

- ✓ *Pot-limit with a maximum bet cap.* In this scenario, the maximum bet is the size of the pot, but not more than a certain amount.
- ✓ *Half pot-limit.* In this game, players may bet up to half the pot at any time.
- ✓ *Pot-limit to no-limit.* In this game, the betting is structured as pot-limit before the flop but changes to no-limit after the flop. Therefore, during play, pot-limit rules apply prior to the flop and no-limit rules apply once the flop is exposed.

5.5 SPREAD-LIMIT POKER

Spread-limit poker is typically found in lower-limit games, such as $1–$4 or $1–$5 seven-card stud and $1–$4–$8–$8 or $2–$10 Texas hold'em. Instead of fixed bets on various betting rounds, payers may wager any amount between the lower and higher limits at any time, as long as all raises are at least the size of the last bet or raise made on that betting round.

INTERPRETATION NOTE

If a player bets $4 in a $2–$10 hold'em game, the next player's options are to fold, call the $4 bet, or raise any amount between $4 and $10, thus raising the pot to between $8 and $14.

Although all raises must be at least the size of the last bet or raise made on that betting round, it all begins again on the next betting round, and players may wager any amount within the spread limits. Excepting all-in situations, the amount of a raise in any given round establishes a minimum for any following re-raises in that same betting round.

When spread-limit games are played with a kill, both the minimum and maximum amounts of the bets are increased.

INTERPRETATION NOTE

When a $2–$10 hold'em game is played with a kill, the stakes will be increased to $4–$20 any time the kill is triggered.

5.6 PLAYING *OVERS*

Playing *overs* is frequently permitted in smaller card rooms to allow players to wager at different stakes than those usually available in small rooms with a limited number of games. When two or more players wish to play for higher stakes, they are said to be *playing overs* or *going the overs*. Overs are usually structured at double the betting limits of the current game, although other multiples may be used.

Overs are in effect on any betting round in which only players who are *going the overs* actively contest the pot. Overs also go into effect any time someone not playing overs is all-in, and only contestants playing overs remain in contention for the side pot.

On the final round of betting, overs become effective when all those not playing overs have folded, even if they were active players at the beginning of that betting round.

ALTERNATE RULE 1: If a player who is not participating in overs is active at any point on the river, overs are not permitted if nonparticipants have folded, but are effective if non-overs participants are all-in.

ALTERNATE RULE 2: Overs are not optional, and are automatically effective when triggered by rule.

ALTERNATE RULE 3: Any player going the overs is also eligible to play *super*-overs, for stakes higher than the overs wagering. Super-overs may include pot- and no-limit betting.

In card rooms with a variety of stakes at different betting limits, overs are not permitted as long as there are games spread at the rough equivalent of the overs stakes.

INTERPRETATION NOTE

Overs usually double the stakes of the game. A $10–$20 game will become $20–$40 when the overs are triggered.

Super-overs are sometimes played pot-limit and even no-limit, such as $15–$30 with $30–$60 overs and pot-limit or no-limit super-overs. A game such as this could also be structured as fixed-limits super-overs. An example would be a game such as $10–$20 to $20–$40 overs, to $30–$60 or $40–$80 super-overs.

However, in a card room that offers games at $10–$20, $20–$40, and higher, there is no reason to attach overs to a $10–$20 game.

5.7 KILL POTS

All games that involve a blind, such as Texas hold'em and Omaha/8, can be played with a *kill*, which has the effect of *doubling* the stakes for the next hand once the kill has been triggered. In the case of a *half-kill*, the stakes will be raised 50 percent for the following hand. Any game played with a kill should have a sign at the table identifying it as such, along with a "kill button" [see Rule 5.29.6] used for identifying when a kill is under way. The kill button itself is used to designate the player responsible for posting the *kill blind*.

5.8 KILL-POT TRIGGERS

Kills are triggered by a specific event, such as winning two hands in a row, scooping the high and low portions of the pot in a high-low split-pot game, or by winning a pot in excess of some predetermined threshold amount. The player who triggers the kill—the *killer*—must post an additional blind on the next hand that is twice the amount of the normal big blind. This effectively doubles the stakes for the next hand, and the betting limits during the kill pot are doubled. If the killer wins this doubled-stakes pot, he continues to kill the pot by again posting a kill blind for the following hand. In effect, the stakes remain doubled until a different player wins, at which time the stakes revert to the normal limits for that game.

Some seven-stud/8 games are played with an "action button," which is not a kill, but is often referred to as a kill pot in error. [See Rule 7.4.2 for a discussion of *action button* usage.]

5.9 KILLING POT FROM BLINDS

In games like hold'em and Omaha—that feature blind bets instead of antes—the killer gets a "discount" on the kill whenever he is in the blind. He is still required to post a kill that effectively doubles the stakes for the ensuing hand, but

INTERPRETATION NOTE

In a $4–$8 game (which typically has blinds of $2 and $4), a player killing the pot must post a third blind in the amount of $8, and the stakes for the ensuing hand are $8–$16. If the killer wins the pot, the stakes stay at $8–$16, with the killer continuing to post a third blind, called a kill.

If the same game was played with a half-kill, the stakes would increase from $4–$8 to $6–$12 whenever an event occurred that triggered the kill.

the required kill is not posted on top of his normal blind. *The kill is posted instead of the player's normal blind.* The player in the other blind position posts the same amount that he would normally post. If the pot is not raised, then the other blind—the one that did not kill the pot—must fold, call the kill amount, or raise when the action returns to him.

5.10 LEG UP

When there is no kill, the winner of a pot is given the kill button face down, and is said to have a *leg up*. The inverted kill button will remain in front of the preceding hand's winner as long as he is active in the subsequent hand, but can be returned to the dealer if the player folds during this subsequent hand's play. If the player possessing the leg up (inverted kill button) wins this next hand, thereby triggering a kill, he will turn the kill button face up, so that the word

INTERPRETATION NOTE

If Scott is the big blind in a $4–$8 game and has to kill the pot, he posts a blind of $8. If Heather is in the small blind, she posts her normal $2 blind, and can either call the difference ($6) between her small blind and Scott's initial $8 kill, fold her hand, or raise when the action gets back to her. This assumes no other players have raised, but if others have, then she would have to also meet the additional raise amounts in order to continue in the hand, by calling or re-raising herself.

If Heather is the killer, then she would post an $8 kill blind instead of her normal $2 small blind, while Scott would post his normal $4 big blind. Either way, the killer gets a discount of sorts when killing the pot from either of the blind positions.

"kill" is visible, and post a blind equal according to the *kill blind* rules above.

In most casinos, if the second pot—the one that would trigger the kill—is split due to a tie, the pot is still killed by the player who has now won one pot outright and tied the next one.

ALTERNATE RULE: If a leg-up player splits the next pot, it does not trigger a kill, but the kill button remains face down with that player, who still has a leg up for the ensuing hand.

If there is no kill, a player splitting the pot does not get a leg-up button.

INTERPRETATION NOTE

If Rick already has a leg up but splits the following hand's pot with Stan, it does not trigger a kill; however, Rick still retains the leg up for the next hand. If Barbara won the previous hand (giving her a leg up), but Rick and Stan split the current pot, then neither Rick nor Stan has a leg up, and Barbara returns the kill button to the dealer.

5.11 HIGH-LOW SPLIT GAMES PLAYED WITH KILL

In high-low games played with a kill, a player who wins both the high and low portions of the pot must kill the following pot whenever the current pot reaches a threshold amount, usually five times the big blind. A wager made but not called is *not* considered part of the pot for determining whether the kill threshold has been reached.

INTERPRETATION NOTE

In a $4–$8 game, if the pot totals $40 or more (not counting any final, uncalled wager) and has been scooped, the winner must post a kill of $8 on the next hand, and the betting limits increase for that hand to $8–$16.

5.12 SEQUENCE OF ACTION WHEN POT KILLED

When a pot is killed, action begins to the big blind's left, regardless of where the killer is seated. Players may fold, call the kill, or raise. They may not call the normal big blind, even if the killer is seated to their left. If the killer is to the immediate left of the big blind, and the three blinds are posted sequentially, then action begins to the killer's left. The killer's blind is live, and he may raise when it is his turn to act.

ALTERNATE RULE: Action begins to the killer's left, instead of to the left of the big blind. He acts last on the first betting round, and his blind is live, so he may raise it if he so chooses.

5.13 REFUSAL TO POST KILL

A player refusing to post a kill will be ejected from the game, and not permitted to return for a minimum of two hours.

If a player should have posted a kill but didn't, that player must kill the next pot that does not qualify for a kill. This player must kill the pot even if she chooses to be dealt out or quits the game. Any player failing to post a required kill will not be dealt a hand until the kill is posted.

5.14 DEALER REQUIREMENTS IN ANNOUNCING KILL POTS

Dealers are required to announce to the table that a kill is in effect. This prevents a player from thinking he is raising, when he is merely calling the kill. A player who has called the lesser (normal) blind because he is unaware of a kill *must* call the proper amount. He may not withdraw his bet. The exception to the dealer announcing a kill is in the following rule, regarding *two* and *kill* lowball games.

Kill blinds are considered part of the pot for purposes of determining the size of the pot in pot-limit games.

Blinds may never be chopped in a kill-pot game.

5.15 LOOK-AT-TWO-AND-KILL (IN LOWBALL GAMES)

In some lowball games, players are permitted to kill the pot after looking at their first two cards. Once a third card is dealt to any player, the pot may no longer be killed. To *look at two and kill*, a player is required to have a minimum of four times the amount of the kill in his stack.

INTERPRETATION NOTE

In a $4–$8 game, the "look at two" killer must have at least $32 in chips before being allowed to post a voluntary kill. This rule is used in conjunction with a structure that allows the killer to act last on the first betting round, rather than in normal sequence.

5.16 HALF-KILLS

Rather than using a full kill, which causes the stakes to double when a kill is required, games may be designated as "half-kill." In *half-kill* games, the amount of the kill blind becomes 150 percent of the big blind and the stakes are effectively raised by 50 percent whenever the pot is killed.

INTERPRETATION NOTE

A \$10–\$20 half-kill game requires a kill blind of \$15 to be posted when the kill is activated. The half-killed hand is played at stakes of \$15–\$30.

5.17 VOLUNTARY KILLS AND LIVE STRADDLES

In most card rooms, voluntary kills are prohibited. A voluntary kill occurs when, if no player at the table objects, the pot may be voluntarily killed by any player if it has not already been killed by another player. To do this, the player voluntarily killing the pot must announce that he is doing so, and post his kill blind prior to any cards being dealt. A player posting a voluntary kill always has the option to raise. A voluntary straddle is accepted in more card rooms. The straddle occurs when a player under the gun posts a raise as a blind bet. It is a "live" bet in that this player has the option to raise after the big blind.

ALTERNATE RULE: Voluntary kills will be permitted.

5.18 HAND SHOWDOWN ORDER

When the last card has been dealt and all the betting is done, the dealer asks the players still active in the hand to *show down* their hands by turning their cards face up on the table. The pot is awarded to the best hand, based on the

INTERPRETATION NOTE

Voluntary kills differ from straddles in this manner: a kill doubles the stakes; a straddle does not.

Only one kill is permitted per hand, and a player may not voluntarily "overkill" the pot by doubling the first killer's blind. In some card rooms that allow a live straddle, a player sitting right after the live straddler may re-straddle by adding yet another blind raise.

rules of that game. If it is a split-pot game, then the best high hand and the best qualifying low hand will split the pot. If there is no qualifying low hand, the high hand wins the entire pot. If one player has both the best high and low hands, he wins—or *scoops*—the entire pot.

On the final betting round, the last player who actively bet or raised the pot (and was then called) is required to show his hand first. Once he shows his hand, other players reveal their down-cards in clockwise order. If all the remaining players check on the final round, the showdown begins with the player who is seated to the left of the dealer in community-card games such as hold'em and Omaha, and the player whose board requires him to act first in stud games.

Regardless of which player might be *required* to show his or her hand down first, any player who thinks he or she has the winning hand can speed things up immeasurably by immediately turning his or her hand face up. Any player with a better hand may then turn his or her hand over.

INTERPRETATION NOTE

On the final round of betting, Michael bets, Philip raises, and Quinn re-raises, only to find that he is called by both Michael and Philip. As the last raiser, Quinn is required to show down his hand first. He will be followed in turn by Michael, who is to the left of Quinn, and finally by Philip, who is to the left of Michael.

Because *cards speak*, players should take care not to relinquish their hands until all the hands that are contesting the pot are turned face up. While a verbal declaration from a player who says, "I fold," is tantamount to mucking his hand, a statement such as "You win," or "My hand can't possibly win," will not be construed as a fold.

While statements like this are clearly unethical and reek of *angle-shooting*, cards still speak and any player thinking she has a chance to win the pot should take care to protect her hand at all times by turning it face up on the table, rather than assuming the pot is hers, and flipping her cards face down toward the muck while an opponent still holds cards in his hand.

The player holding the winning hand should release her cards to the dealer as the dealer pushes the pot toward her.

INTERPRETATION NOTE

It can be very frustrating to watch two or more players sit there, each waiting for another to turn his hand over. Although none of these players feels very strongly about his hand, it's a lot better for the game if someone—anyone—turns his hand over. No matter what, cards speak. Once a hand has been revealed, then the other active players can speed things up by either turning their own hands face up (if they can beat what's already been revealed), or tossing them into the muck, thus allowing everyone to mercifully move on to the next hand. Remember, though, that by tossing your cards unseen into the muck, you forfeit any right to win the hand in the odd instance where you misread your own holdings. Therefore, simply turning your cards face up at showdown is the safest action.

❋❋❋❋❋❋❋❋❋❋❋❋❋

Sheree Bykofsky reports this story from a local club.

TOPIC
Cards Speak: The Case of the "You Win" Declaration

A was an aggressive player who bluffed a lot. M was usually a very tight and conservative player. On the river, A bet and M called. Instead of revealing his cards as he was to do so first, having made the

bet on the river, A said to M, "You win," but he held on to his cards upside down as if to toss them away. The caller, M, asked "Are you sure I won?" A, the aggressor, said, "Yes," and kept holding his cards toward the dealer who didn't take them from him as they were never released. The caller, M, said, "Okay," and flipped up his cards to shockingly reveal a six-high. The dealer sent the chips to the six-high as the aggressor turned over a jack-king no pair and the floor came over and agreed it was the right ruling. In a club like this, saying "You win" means you have forfeited the right to win the hand.

Most casinos would have ruled differently, saying cards speak. If A did not release his hand, he was entitled to flip up his king-high and claim the pot with the better hand.

Assessment

What M should have done instead of asking, "Are you sure," was say, "Show your hand or muck it." Once A's cards were mucked, then M could claim the pot legitimately and irretrievably. If a player at the table then called to see a winning hand, M would have then had to reveal his six-high, thus showing that he had made a mind-blowing call. After all, the only way he could have won that hand would have been if A refused to show his cards, which perhaps M counted on, or if he psychicly knew that A was going to say, "You win," and the house would rule the declaration a muck.

5.19 ALL CARDS MUST BE SHOWN DOWN

To win the pot, all the cards in a player's hand must be shown face-up on the table.

ALTERNATE RULE: Only those cards used to make the best five-card poker hand must be turned face up.

INTERPRETATION NOTE

Some casinos have this rule but it's not very common, and in the interests of rule standardization, the alternate rule is not recommended. Cards speak. Allow them to.

5.20 ASKING TO SEE A WINNING HAND

If, on the last round of betting, all players muck their hands except one, the pot may be shipped to the last remaining player without that player revealing her cards. But if any player at the table requests to see the winning hand, the dealer must reveal the winner's holdings before the winning hand is mucked.

5.21 POT-SPLITTING ON TIE HANDS (AWARDING ODD CHIPS)

If two or more hands are identical, they tie and the pot—or that portion of the pot in split-pot games—is divided equally among those players. Any odd chip should be broken down to the smallest denomination used in that game [see Rule 2.40]. Whenever two or more hands tie, an odd chip will be awarded to the hand immediately to the left (clockwise) of the button in flop games such as hold'em or Omaha.

In high-only stud games, the odd chip should be awarded to the high card by suit; in high-low split games, it should be awarded to the high hand; and in low-only stud games such as razz, to the low card by suit. As with the main pot, all side pots should be split as though they were separate pots and not mixed together before splitting.

5.22 PLAYERS' OBLIGATIONS IN DETERMINING BEST HAND AT SHOWDOWN

Although the dealer is required to determine the best hand and award the pot accordingly, cards speak, and every player at the table has an ethical obligation to speak up if he notices a dealer error. A player holding what he believes to be the winning hand should retain his hand until the pot is awarded. A player with an interest in the pot should not release his hand until the dealer pushes the pot, or his portion of the pot, to him.

5.23 MISCALLED HANDS

Any player who deliberately miscalls as a ploy to induce an opponent to discard his hand is unethical. The player committing this breach of etiquette should forfeit his interest in the pot, although the decision ultimately is made by the floor supervisor, not the dealer.

INTERPRETATION NOTE

You'll occasionally hear players say they don't want to comment on awarding a pot in which they are not involved. This is wrong, and violates one of poker's cardinal ethics. You are not violating *omerta*, going against a police department's code of silence, or acting as a schoolyard tattler by pointing out the winning hand. It's what you should do. Anything else is unethical and against the traditions of the game. Remember: cards speak. Always. However, do not comment on a player's holdings if that player has not placed his cards face up on the table.

Holding on to your hand until the pot is awarded is analogous to that time-honored admonition given by the referee to boxers when he says, "Protect yourself at all times." At the poker table, you're admonished to "Protect your hand at all times." If you think you have the winning hand, hang on to it until the dealer can read your hand and determine which player is entitled to the pot. If you have a question, have him explain the superiority of the hands in play. It's his job.

5.24 ORDER OF AWARDING POTS

Side pots—created when one or more players go all-in during a hand and wagering continues between remaining players—are always awarded first. If there is more than one side pot, they are awarded in order from most recently created to the oldest. The main pot is awarded last.

5.25 PLAYERS' RIGHTS TO SEE CALLED HANDS

Any participant in a hand may ask to see a hand that was called. The proper dealer procedure is to kill the called hand by touching it to the muck, then place the hand face up on the table. If the player who won the pot asks to see the mucked hand, and the mucked hand is actually the superior hand, then the caller's hand is assumed to be live and the pot will be awarded to that player. If a third party asks to see a called hand, the called hand is considered dead. Even if it turns out to be the better hand, it is dead and cannot claim the pot.

INTERPRETATION NOTE

A continual request to see hands is a breach of poker etiquette. However, occasionally allowing players to see called hands protects them against collusion, and that's the goal of this rule. When the rule is bent to the point that it is applied solely to get a read on an opponent's playing style, or worse yet, to annoy and irritate him, it becomes an ethical violation and contrary to the traditions of the game.

ALTERNATE RULE: Any player who has been dealt in may ask to see any hand that has been called, even if the opponent's hand or the winning hand has been mucked. *However, the requesting player must be able to substantiate the reason for asking to see a hand.*

INTERPRETATION NOTE

By requiring that a player have a valid reason for asking to see a called hand, this advances the principle behind the "any hand, any time" precept. Such a requirement polices players who repeatedly breach etiquette by requesting to see hands too often.

This "O'Malley Rule," as it's called, is a new rule suggested by poker manager Mike O'Malley. It is stronger than the traditional rule, and, in your authors' opinion, long overdue. We recommend its adoption.

5.26 SHOW ONE, SHOW ALL

Any time a player shows his hand to another player at the table, all other players at the table—regardless of involvement in the pot—have the right to see the hand, and it is the dealer's obligation to show it.

INTERPRETATION NOTE

"Show one, show all" is part of poker's heritage, and is fair as well as ethical.

❋❋❋❋❋❋❋❋❋❋❋❋

The following story is from Sheree Bykofsky.

TOPIC
Show One, Show All: The Case of the Biased Dealer and the Slippery Player

Sheree is an enthusiastic proponent of the "show one, show all" rule. On her very first visit to the poker room of a particular casino in Las Vegas, Sheree sat down in a one-two no-limit hold'em game where most of the players knew each other. In situations like this one, the newcomer is at a disadvantage because most other players know who is tight, who is weak, who makes tough lay downs and who plays any two cards. Two hands into the game, a player went all-in and the player in the No. 10 seat next to the dealer couldn't decide whether to call. He held his cards way up in the air and angled them to the dealer to show the dealer what a hard decision he had to make. He held his cards there for several seconds. While he agonized, the player in the No. 1 seat on the other side of the dealer got a good look at the cards, and the player in the No. 2 seat got a quick peek, too. Sheree asked the dealer to reveal those cards if the player folded. The player folded, and the dealer refused to expose those cards. Sheree asked the player in the No. 1 seat to admit that he had seen the cards. The player said, "I didn't look." As the floor was called over, the No. 1 seat added, "but that doesn't mean I didn't see the cards. I didn't say I didn't see the cards, but I wasn't in the hand." (Sheree saw him see the cards while the dealer was looking at the cards.) The No. 2 seat, who was even farther from the cards in question, admitted to getting a quick peek at the cards. The dealer gave what Sheree thinks was his biased view of the situation to the floor supervisor who determined that Sheree had no right to see the No. 10 seat's cards. Sheree had to accept the rule but later calmly told the floor supervisor she disagreed with his decision. The floor supervisor cut Sheree off in the middle of her appeal. Later, he wished her a nice evening.

Lesson

When some players at the table are privy to more information than other players, it adds an unnecessarily unfair aspect to the game. New players are already at a disadvantage in a home game, and sometimes players at the table are married, in relationships, or share income. Every effort should be made to level the playing field so that the game may be played in an atmosphere of good gamesmanship. That is why the "show one, show all" rule is important. Players who do not want the whole table to see their cards should muck them whenever they have the right to do so and show them to nobody.

5.27 NON-CORRECTABLE ERRORS

Once the dealer has begun to shuffle the deck for the next hand, all rights to revisit decisions regarding the previous hand have expired, with the exception of decisions that are to be predicated on a review by security cameras. When this happens, the pot is held is escrow, and awarded based on information recorded by security cameras.

5.28 JACKPOTS

Jackpots are more a part of poker marketing than poker itself, but are common promotional tools, particularly in games with betting limits of $10–$20 or less. A sum of money, typically $1 per hand, is taken from each pot and contributed to the jackpot pool. This jackpot pool is collected separately from the rake.

The jackpot pool is accounted for separately, and used to pay players who make hands that trigger the awarding of the jackpot. Jackpot-triggering events could include the high hand for the day, any royal flush, or a bad-beat jackpot that takes place when one very good hand—such as aces full or four-of-a-kind—loses to an even bigger hand.

In some states—California, Nevada, and New Jersey among them—special "jackpot" laws regulate the administration of a casino's rules.

5.28.1 HIGH-HAND AND ROYAL FLUSH JACKPOTS

Some casinos and card rooms distribute jackpot money through a payout for each day's high hand and/or for any royal flush. Because bigger hands typically occur in Omaha

INTERPRETATION NOTE

We recommend that all casinos inform their players about jackpot administration procedures, including the percentage of the jackpot drop going into the jackpot fund, even when not required by law.

than in hold'em or stud games, most casinos that offer a variety of games establish separate jackpots for hold'em, stud, and Omaha games.

For casinos that offer both high-hand and royal flush jackpots, 75 to 80 percent of each day's accumulation is typically awarded to that day's high hand, with the remainder continuing to build separately until a player hits a royal flush. Because a royal flush (best hand possible) is always a winner in the daily high-hand jackpot, a player making a royal flush wins both the royal flush jackpot and daily high-hand jackpot with the same hand, unless two or more players hit royal flushes on the same day. Tied jackpots of either type should be divided equally.

5.28.2 BAD-BEAT JACKPOTS

If offered, the casino has the obligation to post the rules governing its bad-beat jackpots. This information should include the amount of money contributed from each pot, the minimum qualifying hands for awarding the jackpot, how many cards from the player's own hand must be used, and the amount of administrative fees taken from the jackpot. These rules should also specify whether employees are eligible for any jackpot promotions. If video surveillance is required prior to making a jackpot payout, notification of this requirement should also be included in the posting.

The jackpot totals for each game should be updated and posted daily, as well as the sum available for a "backup" jackpot, in the event the jackpot is hit during that day's play. These figures represent the payout totals for the casino's jackpots until the posting is updated the following day. Here is a typical and appropriate division of a jackpot:

✓ Losing hand: 50%
✓ Winning hand: 25%
✓ Table share (distributed among remaining active players who played that hand): 25%

If two players take a bad beat, the allocation is typically:

✓ Best losing hand: 30%
✓ Second-best losing hand: 25%
✓ Winning hand: 20%
✓ Table share (distributed among remaining active players who played that hand): 25%

ALTERNATE RULE: Sometimes the whole room is awarded a share of the jackpot.

5.28.3 JACKPOT QUALIFIERS AND CONDITIONS

Four players must be dealt into the hand for it to qualify for a jackpot. Separate jackpots should be maintained for hold'em, stud, and Omaha games, and games that do not participate in the jackpot will not have a jackpot drop taken.

While each casino can set jackpot qualifiers to suit their

own marketing needs, typical hands that trigger a jackpot event are as follows:

- ✓ In seven-card stud, losing with four-of-a-kind or better qualifies as a bad beat.
- ✓ In Texas hold'em, aces full of tens or better are beaten by four-of-a-kind, as long as both cards in each player's hand are used to construct the best possible five-card poker hand. If the player's side card ties the board card to produce a jackpot hand, it qualifies.
- ✓ In Omaha games, losing with four-of-a-kind or better qualifies as a bad beat.

A player who mentions that a bad-beat jackpot situation is possible has violated the one-player-per-hand rule, which may void the awarding of the jackpot. A decision to void a jackpot will be based on a determination of facts and circumstances by the floor supervisor.

Video surveillance tapes will be reviewed before any jackpot is awarded. In the United States, any player receiv-

---

INTERPRETATION NOTE

Jackpots are seldom disallowed. After all, the jackpot winner usually tokes the dealer and floor supervisor, so they have a vested interest in seeing that it's awarded. Nevertheless, our advice to you is not to push your luck. Avoid talking about a potential jackpot while a hand is in play. Loose lips have been known to sink ships.

ing an amount exceeding the minimum required for IRS reporting must provide a photo ID, such as a driver's license or passport, along with his Social Security number. Appropriate IRS forms should be given to each player at the time he is awarded his jackpot money, which occurs after the player's documentation is recorded.

Jackpot awards that do not meet IRS reporting requirements do not require the casino to procure the player's Social Security number or photo ID.

5.29 BUTTONS

In addition to the large-size dealer button, a variety of other buttons are typically employed in poker games. Their uses are varied and may be used to serve notice that a player has missed the blinds, is absent from the table, has a seat locked up, has given money to an attendant and is awaiting delivery of chips—called *playing behind*—or that players are *going the overs*. Buttons are also used to denote a kill or a leg up on a kill, to indicate a pending request for a seat change, and to indicate *action* in a seven-stud/8 game.

An *absent* or *no player* button indicates a player is away from the table. It is usually white or blue, though the color of the button has no significance within play.

A *lock-up* or *reserved* button indicates that a player must secure either the floor supervisor's permission, or the permission of whichever person is responsible for player interest and waiting lists.

5.29.1 MISSED BLIND BUTTON

This button indicates the player has missed both of his blinds. Any player missing his big blind is required to wait until the button passes him and then post a live big blind and a dead small blind behind the button, or else sit out an entire round until he is once again in the big blind.

Not all casinos use a button to designate that a player has missed his blinds.

5.29.2 SMALL BLIND BUTTON

This button is used to indicate that a player has missed only her small blind, not both of them. Whenever a missed small blind is posted, it is dead. A player who moves out of the small blind is required to post it in her new seat.

In pot-limit and no-limit games where three blinds are posted (the third blind is posted on the button), a player who missed the small and middle blinds may reenter play by posting one big blind. This is conditioned on the fact that a player in this situation will not be dealt a hand on the button. Instead, the button passes to the player's left. This player receives the button instead of the player who reentered play by posting. However, the player who has been given the button must also post a blind if it is necessary to meet the requirement of *three blinds* per hand.

5.29.3 OVERS BUTTON

Each player who is *going the overs* is given a button indicating his participation. If some players are going the overs and others are playing *super*-overs, those playing superovers are usually given two "overs" buttons to distinguish them from others who are merely playing the overs.

5.29.4 PLAYING BEHIND BUTTON

This is a seldom-used button that indicates a player has more money in play than is actually in front of him. It most often occurs when a player first sits down and has given money to an attendant who is in the process of bringing chips to the table. It can also appear on the table whenever a player re-buys and must await delivery of his chips.

Rather than using a button, most card rooms simply announce the amount that a player is playing behind.

INTERPRETATION NOTE

If John has $50 in front of him, but has given $100 to a chip attendant who is currently fetching his chips, the dealer will announce, "Seat Four is playing $100 behind."

5.29.5 OPENERS BUTTON

This is an occasionally seen button, used to denote the pot's opener in a draw-poker game that has a *qualifier,* such as jacks-or-better, to open the betting.

5.29.6 KILL BUTTON

Kill buttons are employed to indicate a player who has a *leg up* as well as to indicate when a player must post a *kill.* If the requirement for killing the pot is winning two pots in a row, a player winning a pot receives the kill button turned face down, signifying that he won the last pot. If he wins the next pot, he is required to turn the button face up and post a kill, which indicates to the table that the stakes have doubled for the following hand.

5.29.7 SEAT-CHANGE BUTTON

Some casinos use these buttons to track the players who have requested seat changes, and the order in which the requests were made. They're not all that common, but seat-change buttons can reduce the confusion in determining which player has highest priority for a seat change.

INTERPRETATION NOTE

Casinos using seat-change request buttons usually have three at each table, labeled "First Seat Change," "Second Seat Change," and "Third Seat Change." When two or more players request a seat change, these buttons provide an accurate record of prioritized requests.

5.30 TABLE CARD

Each table will have a card, placard, or other signage indicating the game being played, the betting limits, the minimum permissible buy-in, and the rake or time collection for that game.

♥ ♠ ♦ ♣

PART THREE

Rules
of the
Games

♦ ♣ ♥ ♠

CHAPTER 6

TEXAS HOLD'EM, OMAHA, AND OTHER COMMUNITY-CARD (BOARD) GAMES

Aside from draw and lowball games, which have declined in popularity in recent years, most poker games fall into one of two types. Many games are variants of stud poker, in which each player has his own cards. Others are games like Texas hold'em or Omaha—games that are characterized by each player receiving some private cards face down. These cards are each player's to see alone, whereas the communal or community cards are displayed face up in the center of the table. In these games, the communal (face-up) cards are available to all, working in conjunction with each player's down cards to construct potentially winning five-card poker hands.

6.1 TEXAS HOLD'EM

Texas hold'em uses five community cards—collectively referred to as the *board*—and each player receives two private cards. Each player seeks to form the best five-card poker hand that can be made using any combination of his two private cards and the five board cards.

While public card rooms always employ five board cards, variations can be found in home games where more community cards are employed, and there is no shortage of the number of permutations that can be created from various private-card and communal-card combinations, as well as the placement of the communal cards—which can be arrayed into three separate boards, boards with criss-cross patterns, and other unique placements.

6.1.1 DEALING AND BETTING PROCEDURES

The game commences with two blinds posted to the left of the dealer position. Two hole cards are dealt face down to each player, which is followed by a round of wagering. In fixed-limit games, a bet and either three or four raises are permitted per betting round, unless the round begins with only two active players. In that case, there is no limit on the number of raises.

Once the first round of wagering is complete, the dealer burns a card and deals three cards in the center of the board. These three cards are known as the *flop*. Once the flop is exposed, another round of betting takes place.

When betting on the flop has been equalized, the dealer burns another card before dealing a single card to the board. This is called the *turn card,* or simply, the *turn*. This is followed by another round of betting. In fixed-limit games, betting limits usually double on the turn. As in all rounds, a bet and three or four raises are allowed.

Once betting on the turn has been equalized, the dealer burns and deals the final board card, known as the *river*. A final betting round takes place, and if there is more than one active player at the conclusion of the wagering, a *show-down* determines the best five-card poker hand.

Hold'em games, in summary, feature two private cards that are dealt to each active player, five communal cards shared by all players, and a pot that is built through the course of four betting rounds.

Typical structures for fixed-limit and spread-limit hold'em, Omaha, and other community card games are as follows:

Stakes	Big Blind	Small Blind	Minimum Buy-in	Smallest Chip Used in Game
$2-to-$10*	$2	$1	$40	$1
$4-to-$20*	$4	$2	$80	$1
$1–$4–$8*	$1	$1	$40	$1
$3–$6	$3	$2	$30	$1
$6–$12	$6	$4	$60	$1
$10–$20	$10	$5	$100	$5
$15–$30	$15	$10	$150	$5
$20–$40	$20	$10	$200	$5
$30–60	$30	$20	$500	$5
$40–$80	$40	$20	$800	$5
$50–$100	$50	$25	$1,000	$25
$75–$150	$75	$50	$1,500	$25

* = spread-limit games.

6.1.2 ORDER OF PLAY

A dealer button—a flat, usually white puck with the word "dealer" often emblazoned on it—determines the order of the deal and action for each hand. This disk is used to designate the player who would be the dealer for that hand, if the game were dealt by the players themselves and not by a house dealer. Cards are dealt in clockwise fashion, beginning with the player to the immediate left of the dealer button. The player in the dealer position is the last to receive cards on the initial deal, and acts last on each betting round with this exception: On the first round of betting, the two players to the dealer's immediate left—who had to post blind bets before seeing their hands—get to act after the dealer. For this initial action, the first betting decision regarding the hand belongs to the player to the left of the big blind, often referred to as *under the gun*.

6.1.3 BLIND BETS

The blind bets are the initial chips posted by the two players to the immediate left of the dealer (the small and big blinds, respectively). These chips seed the pot, and all action begins as a chase for the blinds. In limit games, blinds are usually structured as follows: The player to the immediate left of the dealer posts a "small blind" of anywhere between one-third and two-thirds of a small bet. The "big blind" seated to the immediate left of the small blind posts a blind equal to one small bet.

The chips most frequently in use during the game often determine the blind structure. For example, in a $10–$20 game that uses $5 chips, blinds are typically $5 and $10. But in a $15–$30 game that uses the same $5 chips, the blinds are typically $10 and $15.

Except for the occasional "pink chip game," which employs $2.50 chips, most casinos don't have chips in fractional denominations over one dollar.

Most online poker rooms seek to replicate the experience of brick-and-mortar casinos and structure blinds just as one would find them in the real world. So even though $7.50 and $15 chips could easily be created for cyber poker rooms, you'll generally find $10 and $15 blinds in online $15–$30 poker games.

As mentioned above, the player under the gun (to the immediate left of the big blind) begins the hand's betting. He has the option of folding, calling the big blind, or raising. Acting in clockwise rotation, each player may then fold, call any bets or raises, or raise the pot. If the number of allowable raises has been reached on any given round, players who have yet to act may fold or call the final raise in order to match all previous bets.

On subsequent wagering rounds, action begins with the first active player to the button's left, who may check or bet. If he checks, the next active player to his left has the same options. Once someone bets, players who act after the bettor may fold, call, or raise, until a cap on raising has been reached and the betting has been equalized.

6.1.4 BUILDING HANDS

Each player receives two hole cards, which can be combined in any fashion with the five community cards to build the best possible five-card poker hand. [Hand rankings are listed in Rule 4.8.] Any player may use zero, one, or two cards from his hand in combination with the communal cards to form the best possible five-card hand, and the remaining two cards—whether hole cards or from the board—do not play for that player. Even if two hands are tied, the ranks of the sixth and seventh cards are irrelevant: each player's poker hand comprises five cards and five cards only.

A player who uses no cards from his hand and constructs his hand from the five communal cards on the board is said to be *playing the board*. Anyone playing the board at the showdown is required to declare his intention, then turn his two private hole cards face up on the table. A player who plays the board can only tie for the best hand or lose the pot; he cannot be an outright winner.

Any player throwing his hand away before showing it, even if he has declared that he is playing the board, will forfeit his interest in the pot if his cards hit the muck without being turned over. Although a poker hand is constructed from five cards, all of a player's cards must be displayed to win a showdown.

ALTERNATE RULE: Any player may discard his hand face down once announcing his intention to play the board.

6.2 OMAHA HOLD'EM

Two forms of Omaha are played frequently in casinos and card rooms: One is Omaha eight-or-better, high-low split (usually abbreviated as Omaha/8), a split-pot game that's usually played at fixed betting limits. The other, usually referred to as Omaha high, or Omaha high-only, is a game in which the high hand wins the entire pot. Omaha high is usually played with pot-limit betting.

However, the overall betting structure, the blinds, the

"burn-'n'-turn" manner in which the board is dealt, and all of the other procedures in Omaha are the same as they are in Texas hold'em, with just a few exceptions:

6.2.1 NUMBER OF CARDS

Rather than receiving two private cards, as in Texas hold'em, Omaha players receive four private cards.

INTERPRETATION NOTE

In a Texas hold'em game, a player who combines a single heart from his hand with four hearts from among the community cards will have a heart flush. To make a heart flush in Omaha-high or Omaha/8, that player must use exactly two hearts from his hand and exactly three hearts from the board, or he will not have a flush.

You cannot construct a hand with three of your private cards and two community cards, or one private card and four community cards. You must construct your hand—or hands in the case of Omaha/8—by using exactly two private cards and three communal cards. Omaha is the game where hands are most often misread by players, and this simple miscounting of available cards is almost always the reason. Remember, it's two-from-hand-and-three-from-board. Nothing else counts.

6.2.2 BUILDING HANDS

Instead of playing zero, one, or two hole cards as in Texas hold'em, Omaha/8 and Omaha high-only players must form their best five-card poker hand using precisely two cards from their hand and three from the board—no more and no less—in order to build a five-card poker hand.

6.2.3 LOW HANDS MUST "QUALIFY"

In all Omaha/8 games, a low hand must "qualify." A qualified low hand contains five cards of unique rank, each eight

INTERPRETATION NOTE

No low hand is possible in an Omaha/8 game if the board is J-9-8-7-7, or Q-J-9-3-2. A low hand is possible with a board like J-9-7-5-2 or 8-5-3-2-A, but in all cases a player must also have two unique low cards among his four private cards. If the board is J-9-7-5-2, a player holding Q-5-2-A does not have a low hand even though he has three low cards among his four private cards and three low cards are present on the board. Try as he might, he cannot construct a low hand because the five and deuce in his hand have been duplicated—or counterfeited— by the board. If he had a four in his hand instead of the five or the deuce, he would have a low hand.

Try it yourself. See if you can construct a qualifying low hand using two cards from the player's Q-5-2-A, and three from among the J-9-7-5-2 that comprise the board's community cards.

or lower. If no hand qualifies to win the low portion of the pot, then the high hand will scoop the entire pot. Low hands *must* be made up of two low cards from a player's private cards and three low cards from the board. If there are not three unpaired cards with the rank of eight or lower among the community cards, no low hand is possible.

6.2.4 DIFFERING TWO-CARD COMBINATIONS FOR "HIGH" AND "LOW" QUALIFYING HANDS IN OMAHA/8

In Omaha/8, a player may use any two-card combination of his hole cards to make a high hand, a low hand, or both. He may use the same two cards for his high as well as his low hands, or two different cards for each hand, or any two-card combination. But a high hand must use two of his private cards and three from the board and a low hand must be constructed in the same manner. Note that the same private cards can be used to make both the high and low hands.

6.2.5 SHOWING DOWN WINNING HANDS

A player must show all four of his private cards to win any part of the pot, even though some of those private cards almost surely won't be part of the eventual winning hand. The dealer assists all players in reading their hands once the cards have been shown down, correcting any player misreads at that time. Cards speak, and once the showdown occurs, it is the dealer's responsibility and the ethical responsibility of other players at the table to ensure that the best hands win their shares of the pot. If there is a tie for either the high or the low hands, they are divided—and odd

> ### INTERPRETATION NOTE
>
> If the board in an Omaha/8 game is J♦-9♣-6♦-5♦-2♥ and a player holds A♦-K♦-4♣-3♠ in his hand, he will make an ace-high flush by combining his A♦-K♦ with three diamonds from the board. He will also make a six-low by combining the ace and trey in his hand with 6-5-2 from the board to give him 6-5-3-2-A.
>
> He has used the ace of diamonds as a high card (along with his diamond king) to make the highest possible flush, and also used his ace (along with the trey in his hand), in combination with three board cards, to form the best possible low hand.

chips awarded—in exactly the same manner as any other tied pot.

6.2.6 PLAYING OMAHA WITH KILL

Omaha and Omaha/8 are often played with a kill. When the game is Omaha high-only, any player winning two pots in succession is required to kill the subsequent pot. If the game is Omaha/8, any player scooping the pot triggers a kill. In each case, kills are handled as discussed in chapter 5, and a standard killing of the pot doubles the stakes for the next hand. Alternatively, some games are structured as "half-kill" games. In these games, the half-kill raises the next hand's stakes by 50 percent.

INTERPRETATION NOTE

It's not always 50 percent to the penny. While a half-kill $10–$20 game would see an escalation in stakes to $15–$30 if any time a kill is triggered, if the game were $5–$10, the next logical jump would be $8–$16, not $7.50–$15. The reason is simple: casinos don't have $7.50 chips.

6.3 FIVE-CARD OMAHA/8

Occasionally a five-card version of Omaha/8 will be spread in casinos. In this game, each player is dealt five private cards rather than four, but other than that distinction, the game is played identically to the traditional version of Omaha/8 in which each player receives four private cards.

In five-card Omaha/8, players must still use two—and only two—cards from their hand in combination with exactly three of the five community cards to construct the best high and best low poker hands. (And, as always, players may use a different two-from-own/three-from-board combination to construct separate hands for high and low.) As in the standard version of Omaha/8 played with four private cards, the best high hand and best qualifying low hand split the pot.

6.4 THREE-CARD GAMES

Somewhere between Texas hold'em (with its two private cards) and Omaha (with four private cards dealt to each player) is a hybrid land where a few three-card games reside. In each of the games the players receive three private cards, and in each the board is made up of five communal cards, just as in Texas hold'em and Omaha. With a few exceptions noted below, each of these games uses the same rules as Texas hold'em.

6.4.1 PINEAPPLE

Pineapple players are dealt three private cards—one more than the two they'd receive if playing Texas hold'em. Once the three private cards are dealt, there's a round of betting, and after that betting round is complete, each player is required to discard one card to the muck before the dealer burns and turns the flop. After the discard occurs, the game is identical to Texas hold'em.

6.4.2 CRAZY PINEAPPLE

The single difference between pineapple and crazy pineapple is that in crazy pineapple, players discard one of their three private cards to the muck *after* the flop has been dealt. (In pineapple, players discard one of their private cards *before* seeing the flop.) That's it. And once that third communal card has been cast to the muck, crazy pineapple plays like regular pineapple, which in turn plays like plain old Texas hold'em. At that point all the normal hold'em rules apply.

While it's possible to play pineapple—and Texas hold'em, for that matter—as eight-or-better high-low split games, you probably won't find them spread in many casinos. But if you should (or if they should experience a surge in popularity), most of the split-pot rules found in Omaha/8 would apply here as well, with this exception: you could make your best poker hands using zero, one, or two of your private cards, just as you would in Texas hold'em.

6.4.3 TAHOE

Tahoe is another branch of the Texas hold'em tree. Each player is dealt three cards, just as they are in the pineapple games, but there is no discard. As in Texas hold'em, players may use zero, one, or two cards from their hand in combination with the communal cards on the board to form the best five-card poker hand. Players are not permitted to play all three cards from their hands. We suppose this game could have been named Tahoe pineapple, were it not so tough to envision pineapples growing in that climate.

CHAPTER 7

STUD GAMES

Stud games are characterized by the fact that they are "open" poker games. One or more cards are dealt to each player face down, followed by rounds of dealing where cards are dealt face up. In some versions of stud, a final face-down card is dealt to each player. Regardless of the specific stud variation being played, each player receives an entire hand of cards that are his and his alone. There are no community cards as found in games such as Texas hold'em and Omaha.

Stud games can be played for high, for low, and as split-pot games.

In each version of stud, players make their best five-card poker hand from the five, six, or seven cards they are dealt.

7.1 FIVE-CARD STUD

One of the oldest versions of the game is five-card stud, in which players receive one card face down and four cards face up, with a round of betting following each up-card that's dealt. Five-card stud is not as popular as seven-card stud, and although it is available at several online poker sites, it is not spread very frequently in traditional casinos.

A variation of traditional five-card stud is called "one-three-one," where the first and last cards are both dealt face down.

7.2 SIX-CARD STUD

Six-card stud is a form of stud poker in which each player receives two cards face down and one face up, followed by the initial round of betting. Subsequent betting rounds occur after each successive face-up card is dealt, until each player has six cards. In a subtly different version of this game, each player receives one card face down and another face up, followed by a round of betting. A round of betting follows each successive up-card, and the hand concludes with a sixth card dealt face down along with a final round of betting. (The net effect is to add one round of betting to the game.) In both versions, players use the best five of their six cards to construct their best poker hand.

It's also possible to play razz—stud poker played for low—with six cards, but that's a very rare game. Nowadays, razz is played almost exclusively with seven cards.

7.3 SEVEN-CARD STUD

Seven-card stud, which first appeared sometime around the Civil War, is by far the most popular version of stud poker in today's casinos. This game has five rounds of betting. Players receive two cards face down and one face up. This is followed by a round of betting. Each player then receives a fourth card face up followed by another round of betting. The fifth and sixth cards are also dealt face up, and are each followed by a round of betting. The seventh card is dealt face down, and that too is followed by a round of betting. With three down cards and four exposed cards in each player's hand, seven-card stud combines the drama of draw (closed) poker, with a good deal of information that can be gleaned from four open cards. Almost every hand is possible in seven-card stud. This contrasts sharply with games like Texas hold'em, in which full houses or quads (four-of-a-kind) are impossible unless the board contains paired cards, and flushes are impossible unless the board contains three cards of the same suit.

7.3.1 ANTES, DEAL, AND BETTING STRUCTURES

Seven-card stud games have a workable maximum of eight players. Before the cards are dealt, each player posts an ante, which is a fraction of a bet. Since each poker game begins as a chase for the antes, this money seeds the pot. In all games using antes and bring-ins, the ante is *dead* and is not considered part of a player's bet. However, the *bring-in* [see following rule] is *live* and does count as part (or all) of the bring-in player's bet.

During the hand, the dealer is required to announce the low *card* on the initial betting round, the *high* hand on all subsequent betting rounds, and all pairs on board. Dealers do not announce possible straights and possible flushes.

ALTERNATE RULE: Dealers announce possible straights and flushes, along with the low *card* on the initial betting round, the *high* hand on all subsequent betting rounds, and all pairs on board in low-limit games, as a courtesy to inexperienced players.

7.3.2 BRING-INS

Once players have received their three starting cards, the lowest exposed card is *required* to make a partial small bet of a predetermined denomination, called the *bring-in*. The player required to make the bring-in also has the option to bring it in for a complete bet. If two or more players have an exposed card of the same rank, the bring-in is determined by the alphabetical order of suits: clubs, diamonds, hearts, and spades. This tie-breaking procedure is one of the very few times in poker that the order of suits matters.

ALTERNATE RULE: The opener may complete the bet to the full amount of a small bet only if no other player completes the bring-in.

INTERPRETATION NOTE

While the alternate rule induces more action, it is by far the less common method for handling bring-in betting.

7.3.3 BETTING

The player to the immediate left of the bring-in has three options: he may fold his hand, call the bring-in, or raise to a full bet (assuming the bring-in player has not done so already). In a $20–$40 game, the antes are usually $3, and the bring-in is $5. The player to the bring-in's left can fold, call the $5 bring-in bet, or raise to $20–the value of the full small bet in this game.

If he folds or calls the bring-in, the player to his immediate left has the same options. Once someone *completes* to a full bet, subsequent players must fold, call the full bet, or raise. It's important to note that in stud games, the first player to increase the wager on the first betting round can only *complete* the forced bring-in by increasing it to the level of a full bet. However, if the bring-in chooses to start the action at the level of a full bet, then the next player to act has the option of raising.

INTERPRETATION NOTE

If the stakes are $10–$20 and the bring-in is $3, the first player to act may fold, call the bring-in, or complete the bet. But unless the bring-in has chosen to voluntarily bring it in for the full $10 instead of the token $3 wager, the player wishing to raise can only complete the wager to $10, not bump it all the way to $20. A player who completes a forced bet that was less than a full bet is not technically a raiser; he is considered to have completed the bring-in bet. If the house allows a bet and three raises, completing the bring-in is not considered a raise, and three opportunities for raising remain available to other players at the table.

Once betting has been equalized, a second card is dealt face up, and another round of betting ensues. This time, however, it is in increments of full bets. The player with the highest-ranking board cards acts first.

If there are two high cards of the same suit, the order of the suit determines who acts first. The highest suit is spades,

INTERPRETATION NOTE

Doubling the bet whenever the board pairs on fourth street is optional, not mandatory. Any player may elect the double bet, not just the player who has the exposed pair on board.

A player who pairs his door card on fourth street may check or bet either the smaller or larger fixed-limit amount. If the first player to act bets the smaller amount, players acting subsequently may fold, call the small bet, or raise. In a $10–$20 game, if a player makes an open pair on fourth street, any player may bet or raise either $10 or $20, though once a $20 raise has been made, no $10 raises are allowed. Once raised, the stakes cannot revert to wagers of smaller units.

followed by hearts, then diamonds, and finally, clubs. Multiple-card ties, though rare, are resolved in order of the suit of the highest card in the tie.

The first player to act may either check—which, in actuality, is a bet of nothing—or bet. If there is an open pair on board, whether that pair resides in her hand or that of an opponent, then any player has the option to make a big bet, not just the player possessing the open pair.

In fixed-limit games, the first two rounds of betting are small bets. These occur after the first three cards have been dealt and again after the fourth card is dealt (*third street* and *fourth street*). Wagering on fifth, sixth, and seventh streets is done in double-sized or large bets.

In a $20–$40 game, for example, the betting takes place in increments of $20 on fourth street, unless there is an open pair, which creates an option for the bettors. If an open pair shows on fourth street, any bettor may open for either $20 or $40, with all bets and raises continuing in increments consistent with the bet.

Rule 7.3.4, which follows, is a chart containing many recommended and commonly used antes, minimum buy-ins, bring-in bets, and minimum betting units for seven-card stud games played at either fixed or spread limits.

7.3.4 RECOMMENDED BETTING UNITS

Stakes	Ante	Minimum Buy-In	Bring-In	Smallest Chip Used in Game
$1–to$5	0	$20	$1	$1
$5–$10	$0.50	$50	$2	$1
$10–$20	$1	$100	$3	$1
$15–$30	$2	$150	$5	$5
$20–$40	$3	$200	$5	$5
$30–$60	$5	$500	$10	$5
$40–$80	$10	$800	$10	$5
$50–$100	$10	$1000	$20	$5
$75–$150	$15	$1500	$25	$5
$150–$300	$25	$3000	$50	$25

7.3.5 RAISES

Most casinos allow a bet and three or four raises per betting round, except when only two players contest the pot. Then there is no limit to the amount of raises permitted.

In stud, position is determined by the cards showing on the board, and can vary from round to round. With the exception of the first round of betting on third street, where the lowest-ranked card is required to *bring it in,* the highest hand on board acts first, and has the option of checking or betting.

The highest hand could range anywhere from four-of-a-kind to trips, two pair, a single pair, or even the highest card by suit, if no exposed pair is present. Potential straights and flushes do not apply for the purposes of determining the current high hand on the board.

7.3.6 DOUBLE BETS

In fixed-limit games—seven-card stud is predominantly a fixed-limit game—the betting doubles on *fifth street.* Those players still contesting a seven-card stud pot are dealt another exposed card, when the opportunity for doubled bets occurs. Sixth street is the same. The last card, called *seventh street* or *the river,* is dealt face down, but the doubled-bet standard remains in place. At the river, each active player will have a hand consisting of three closed and four open cards. The player who acted first on sixth street is always first to act on seventh street, too.

7.3.7   SHOWDOWNS

If more than one player is active once all betting has equalized, players turn their hands face up, making the best five-card hand from the seven cards they are holding. The player with the best hand wins the showdown.

7.3.8 SPREAD-LIMIT GAMES

Many low-stakes seven-card stud games use spread limits rather than fixed limits, spreading games such as $1–$3 or $1–$4 seven-card stud. These games are frequently played without an ante. The low card is required to bring it in for $1, and all bets and raises can be in increments from $1–$3 or $1–$4—with the provision that all raises be at least the amount of the previous bet. If someone bets $2, the next player to act can fold, call, or raise $2, $3, or $4—but not $1. If the original bettor had wagered $4, the next player in turn can fold, call his $4 bet, or raise to $8.

7.3.9 ORDER OF OPEN CARDS

Purposefully changing the order of up-cards violates the rules and is considered to be cheating in any open poker game because the order of cards dealt can influence betting patterns. Changing the order of up-cards is grounds for immediate expulsion.

7.3.10 MIXING OPEN AND CLOSED CARDS

Turning an open card or cards face down, or commingling open and closed cards together is tantamount to folding. The hand is dead.

7.3.11 ACCIDENTALLY EXPOSING CARDS

Whenever the dealer accidentally exposes a player's first or second hole card, it will be considered an open card and the third card will be dealt face down. If both hole cards are exposed, the player's hand is considered to be dead and his ante shall be returned to him.

If a player has not posted his ante but is dealt a hand in error, it is not a misdeal. Instead, the player should be dealt a complete starting hand, which will immediately be declared dead. If this player would have been the bring-in based on his up-card, the player with the second-lowest open card begins the action.

If the dealer turns the last card face up to any player, the correct procedure depends upon the number of active players in the hand.

With three or more players in the hand, the remaining players will receive their last card face down. Before the last round of wagering commences, the player with the exposed card may partake in the betting or he may opt to be considered all-in. If he chooses the latter, he is ineligible to wager on the final betting round. He is also ineligible to win any bets made on that round. Under these circumstances, bets from other players will comprise a *side pot*.

If only two players are active, and the first player to receive a card has it dealt face up, the second player's final card will also be dealt face up and betting proceeds as normal.

If the first player's card is dealt face down but the second player's card is exposed, that player may choose to be considered all-in. If he chooses this option, no further wagering will take place.

7.3.12 INSUFFICIENT CARDS

If too few cards remain in the deck for all the players to receive a final card, then all the cards except the last card shall be dealt. The last card will be mingled with the burn cards, then scrambled and cut. When this is done, the dealer again burns and deals the remaining down cards.

Though rare, a situation may arise where even the use of burned cards does not yield enough unseen cards to complete the deal on seventh street. Cards from the muck are never reintroduced to the play of the hand. If this procedure does not yield enough cards to enable a final card to be dealt to each player, the burn should be eliminated prior to dealing. If eliminating the burn will still not provide enough cards, the dealer burns a card and turns the next one face up in the center of the table as a community card. The community card plays in the hand of all remaining players. This is the only instance where a community card comes into play in the traditional version of seven-card stud.

When a community card comes into play, seventh-street betting action is initiated by the high hand on the board, including the community card. Because complete five-card hands are now displayed, the traditional order of hand rankings—including four-of-a-kind, full houses, flushes, and straights—determines the betting order.

7.4 SEVEN-CARD STUD, EIGHT-OR-BETTER HIGH-LOW SPLIT (SEVEN-STUD/8)

Seven-card stud, eight-or-better high-low split, abbreviated as seven-stud/8, is a very popular variant of seven-card stud. It is the "E" in the mixed game format of H.O.R.S.E., when players rotate the game being played each orbit around the table among hold'em, Omaha (or Omaha/8), razz, seven-card stud, and seven-stud/8.

7.4.1 QUALIFYING LOW HANDS

All of the rules of seven-card stud apply, except that the high and low hands split the pot. Low hands must *qualify*, and a hand of five unpaired cards with the rank of eight or lower is required to qualify. Straights and flushes do not affect the value of a low hand.

INTERPRETATION NOTE

A hand like 6♦-5♦-4♦-3♦-2♦ would be a straight flush for high, and a six-low for the low hand. The fact that all the cards in the low hand are both sequenced and suited would not count against the low hand.

If the other two cards in this player's hand were the 4♣ and 6♥, the fact that two of his low cards are paired would not count against his low hand either. Because he has five unique cards with the rank of eight or lower, it's a qualifying low hand in addition to a straight-flush for high.

ALTERNATE RULE: Occasionally you'll see a game described as a "no qualifier" game. That's a high-low split game, too, except that a low hand will always be made, because low hands in this format need not qualify.

Each player receives seven cards that can be used in any combination to make hands. Players can make both low and high hands, and win both ends of the pot—called "scooping"—by using five-card combinations of their seven cards to form winning hands for each.

INTERPRETATION NOTE

For example, if Deirdre's cards were A♦ J♦ 9♦ 7♦ 5♦ 4♠ 2♣, her high hand would be an ace-high flush, comprised of A♦ J♦ 9♦ 7♦ 5♦. Her other hand is called a "seven-low," made up of 7♦ 5♦ 4♠ 2♣ A♦. Aces can be used as both the highest and lowest card in the deck.

7.4.2 ANTES, DEAL, AND BETTING STRUCTURES

Seven-stud/8 has five rounds of betting, just like its high-hand-only cousin. Each player posts an ante—which is a fraction of a bet—before the cards are dealt, just as they would in traditional seven-card stud. Antes are used to seed the pot and stimulate action.

Initially, players are dealt two cards face down, along with one face up. The lowest exposed (face-up) card is required to make a small bet of a predetermined denomination, called the *bring-in*. Although an ace can be treated as a low and a high card in this game, it is always considered

INTERPRETATION NOTE

If Joe has the 2♦ and Molly the 2♣, Molly would be required to bring it in based on the order of suits. Molly's 2♣ is the lowest card in the deck, and that card is always the bring-in card when it appears on third street.

to be a high card for purposes of establishing the bring-in, and therefore is almost never the bring-in card. If two or more players have an exposed card of the same rank, the bring-in is determined by the alphabetical order of suits: clubs, diamonds, hearts, and spades.

INTERPRETATION NOTE

In a $20–$40 game, where the antes are usually $3 and the bring-in is $5, the player to the left of the bring-in can fold, call the $5 bring-in bet, or complete the bet to $20—which constitutes a full bet.

The player to the immediate left of the bring-in has three options: fold, call the bring-in, or raise to a full bet.

If the player to the left of the bring-in folds or calls, the same options are available to the next player in clockwise order. Once someone increases the action to a full bet, subsequent players must fold, call the full bet, or raise.

After the betting has equalized, a second card is dealt face up, and another round of betting ensues. This time, however, it is in increments of full bets. The player with the highest-ranking board cards acts first.

If there are two high cards of the same suit, the order of the suit determines who acts first. As always, the highest suit is spades, followed by hearts, then diamonds, and finally, clubs, and the first player to act may either check or bet.

Seven-stud/8 is frequently played with an *action button*. If an action button is used, it comes into play whenever a pot is scooped and exceeds some predetermined amount. When that threshold is met, the winner has to post an *action bet* on the next hand. The action button requires the holder to make a blind raise to increase the action on the next hand.

Although some players informally refer to it as a kill, it is not technically *a kill*, because the stakes do not double. Players who act after the bring-in but before the action button cannot *complete* the bring-in. Instead, they may only call the bring-in if they intend to play. Once the action button's raise becomes effective, they are free to call—or raise—the action bet when it is their turn to act again.

7.4.3 FOURTH STREET—NO DOUBLE BETS

Unlike traditional seven-card stud played for high only, an open pair on board does not afford a player the option of making a double bet in seven-stud/8.

7.4.4 BETTING ORDER

As in seven-card stud played for high, the lowest exposed *card* always acts first on the initial betting round (third street), but the highest exposed *hand* acts first thereafter. Position is always determined by the cards showing on the board and can vary from round to round. With the exception of the first round of betting where *bring-in* rules apply, the highest hand always acts first, and may check or bet.

7.4.5 RAISES

A bet and three or four raises per betting round is the general rule, except when only two players are contesting the pot. As in seven-card stud, completing the bring-in is not considered a raise for purposes of calculating the number of

INTERPRETATION NOTE

In a typical $20–$40 game, the bring-in is $5, and the action button's forced raise is $20. If the bring-in is seated to the dealer's immediate left and the action button is in Seat 5, any players seated to the left of the bring-in and the right of the action button (Seats 2, 3, and 4) may only call the bring-in if they wish to play.

Once the blind (forced) $20 "action" bet comes into play, players to the left of the action button may fold, call the $20 action bet, or raise. When the order of play returns to the bring-in, she and those seated between her and the action button, may act on the forced raise and any subsequent wagering that followed. If no one has re-raised the $20 action bet, the bring-in (and the players whose initial action was limited to just calling the bring-in), now have the full range of wagering options available to them. The action bet is also considered live, and the player who holds the action button will act last on the first round of betting.

permissible raises allowed on the first round of betting. Then there is no limit to the number of raises permitted.

7.4.6 DOUBLE BETS

Betting doubles on *fifth street*, and those players still contesting the pot are dealt another exposed card, followed by a round of betting. Sixth street is the same. The last card, called *seventh street* or *the river,* is dealt face down. At the river, active players have a hand made up of three closed and four exposed cards. The player who acted first on sixth street acts first on seventh street, too.

7.4.7 SHOWDOWNS

If more than one player is active once all betting has equalized, players turn their hands face up in a *showdown,* making the best five-card hand—or hands—from the seven cards they are holding. The best high hand wins half the pot, and the best low hand, assuming there is a qualifying low hand, wins the other half.

> **INTERPRETATION NOTE**
> It's possible for the best high hand and the best low hand to be the same hand. If Shelby holds 6-5-4-3-2 in her hand, she has a six-high straight for a high hand, and a six-low as her low one.

7.5 RAZZ

Razz is seven-card stud played for low only, and the game is played by the same rules as seven-card stud, with some exceptions.

7.5.1 LOW-HAND DETERMINATION

The lowest hand wins the pot, and aces play for low only in this game.

INTERPRETATION NOTE

Because aces are the lowest card in a razz deck, a pair of aces is always lower than a pair of deuces.

7.5.2 BRING-INS

As opposed to other seven-card stud games, in razz the *high* card is required to make the forced bring-in bet, and on subsequent betting rounds the *low* hand always acts first. The highest single card possible—and therefore the worst card, for purposes of razz—is a king. Whenever two players have the same low hand or high single card, suits determine who acts first. For purposes of establishing the lowest card by suit, clubs are lowest, followed by diamonds, then hearts, and finally by spades.

INTERPRETATION NOTE

If, on fourth street, two players each have a five and a trey as their lowest cards, the five of diamonds would act before the five of hearts.

7.5.3 BETTING

In fixed-limit games, betting doubles on fifth street. An open pair on fourth street has no effect on the betting and a double bet is not permitted on that round. Dealers should announce all pairs the first time they occur, although paired face cards should not be announced.

7.6 FIVE-CARD STUD

Although five-card stud is one of the oldest of the stud games, it was moribund for years, and is seldom seen in today's casinos and card rooms. But it has made a modest resurgence as an online game.

All the rules of seven-card stud apply to five-card stud, with some exceptions.

7.6.1 ANTES, DEAL, AND BETTING STRUCTURES

Play begins with an ante posted by each player, who is then dealt one card face down and another face up. The player with the lowest-ranking exposed card has the bring-in, and subsequent players may fold, call the bring-in, or complete it to a full, small bet.

Once the first-round betting has equalized, another card is dealt face up to each player, and betting commences with the player holding the best exposed poker hand. In this and subsequent betting rounds, the player to act first may check or bet up to the game's limit. In fixed-limit games, the betting limits double with the third and fourth exposed cards.

If there is an open pair on the second exposed card, the seven-card stud rules for increasing the limits apply and betting limits may be doubled by any player who elects this option. After the fourth exposed card is dealt, a showdown determines the winner if two or more players are still active.

Five-card stud can also be played as a low game, in which case the bring-in is the highest card showing by suit, but the best low hand showing will begins the action on each subsequent betting round. Five-card stud played for low is, in essence, a five-card version of razz.

It can also be played as a split pot game. In this version, the highest exposed hand acts first.

ALTERNATE RULE: As noted earlier, the fifth and final card may be dealt face down. Whenever the last card is dealt face down, the player acting first on fourth street acts first again on the river.

Although five-card stud is most commonly played at fixed limits, it is also played occasionally as a pot-limit or no-limit game.

7.7 MISSISSIPPI SEVEN-CARD STUD

Mississippi seven-card stud is played exactly like traditional stud poker with two small, but significant, differences:

- ✓ Two cards, rather than just one—think of it as a two-card flop—are dealt before the second betting round begins.
- ✓ The last card is dealt face up rather than face down.

Because the fourth and fifth cards are dealt together rather than separately, this game has only four betting rounds instead of the five that are a feature of traditional seven-card stud.

Though the last card can be dealt either face up or face down in a fixed-limit game, depending on local preferences, whenever Mississippi seven-card stud is played as a pot-limit or no-limit game, the last card should be dealt face up.

7.7.1 DECKS AND DEALING

When Mississippi seven-card stud is played as a fixed-limit game, the low card *brings it in* for a token bet. However, an alternate format applies in the big-bet versions—half-pot, pot-limit, and no-limit. Instead of a token bring-in by the low card, the high card starts the action, and must either bet or fold. He cannot check.

Once the bets and raises on third street have been equalized and the round is complete, each active player receives two additional cards. These cards—fourth and fifth street together—are dealt face up. The highest hand starts the action and may check or bet. Once the betting is concluded, a fourth up-card is dealt and another round of betting ensues. Finally, the river card is dealt face up and final betting occurs.

7.8 MIXED GAMES

Mixed games have grown in popularity in recent years, and are constructed of rounds, in varying combinations, of games such as Texas hold'em, Omaha/8, seven-card stud, seven-stud/8, razz, crazy pineapple, pineapple, and low-ball. The games are known by their acronyms, such as H.O.R.S.E.—(Texas) hold'em, Omaha/8, Razz, seven-card stud, and the "E" which stands for "eight-or-better stud." Other common iterations are R.O.E., H.O.E., C.H.O.R.S.E., and even C.H.O.R.S.E.L., which includes all the H.O.R.S.E games, plus crazy pineapple and lowball are added to the mix.

A table sign is used to indicate which game is in progress and the stakes are the same for all games played.

Each round begins with the player immediately to the

dealer's left and ends with the player on the dealer's right. A button is moved around the table to show the progress of the round. A dealer button is used for games played with a blind, and that button remains with the last player using it even when the game switches to an ante game. Another button should be used in ante games to track the rotation of the deal and the number of hands dealt. When each full table orbit is complete, the game changes to the next one in the rotation.

ALTERNATE RULE: The game is changed every half hour, when a new dealer comes to the table.

INTERPRETATION NOTE

Because games such as lowball, with only two betting rounds, and Texas hold'em play faster than Omaha/8 and seven-card stud, changing games at the end of each table orbit is more equitable than rotating games at the end of each half hour or every time a new dealer comes into the box. Rotation by orbit ensures that each player will be dealt the same number of hands of each game.

7.8.1 BACK MAN OUT

Many mixed games, such as C.H.O.R.S.E., are played with nine or ten players at the table. That's a problem when it comes time to play seven-card stud, razz, or seven-stud/8. When that happens the game is usually played *back man out,* and one player—the one who would be the last player in the rotation—sit the hand out. Because it's rotational in nature, each player sits out one hand during an orbit of stud games. If this procedure is used, a table sign should be posted. The button used to track the orbit of play at the table can also be employed to designate the player who is sitting out.

CHAPTER 8

DRAW AND OTHER GAMES

Draw poker—the game typically shown in Western movies—is much older than its stud and flop game counterparts. Although draw poker has lost much of its luster as a casino game in recent years, it remains popular in home games.

Draw poker is predicated on players replacing some of the five cards they are initially dealt. Players discard some of their cards and draw replacement cards in hopes of improving their hand. Draw is a *closed* poker game, and is a game in which the players conceal all their cards until the showdown. This is very different from both stud and flop games, in which each player has some open and some closed cards and games that feature community cards used by all players in the hand, which are turned face up in the center of the table.

Two rounds of betting are typical in most forms of draw poker, with the exception of triple draw, in which players have three opportunities—rather than one—to muck the cards they don't like and replace them with ones they hope are better.

8.1 DRAW AND LOWBALL WITH JOKER

The winner is decided based on traditional hand values, with this exception: Draw poker games are frequently played with a joker added to the deck as a fifty-third card. It's called a "bug," and though not a wild card per se, the joker can be used in high-hand draw games to complete straights and flushes, or it may be used as an ace. Because of this, the best draw hand is five aces when the game is played with a joker, not the straight flush that tops the ranking in poker games played with fifty-two-card decks. In lowball games, the bug is used as the lowest card not in a player's hand. In these games, it is sometimes referred to as a *fitter*.

8.2 JACKS-OR-BETTER

Back before Texas hold'em was legalized in California card rooms, draw poker and lowball were the only games in town. Draw poker comes in two flavors. In the first, players are permitted to open the betting with any hand; no qualifier is required. But the far more popular version of draw poker was "jacks-or-better," in which a player was required to have a pair of jacks or higher in order to open the betting.

Jacks-or-better has a progressive betting feature. If no player opens the pot with at least a pair of jacks, the button moves forward, everyone must ante once again, and the opening requirement advances to queens or better. Most games allow three consecutive deals before antes stop and the opening requirements are frozen or dropped. [For more details refer to Rule 8.2.3, Order of Play.]

INTERPRETATION NOTE

If no one opens, additional antes will not be required anytime three iterations of dealing have transpired. At that point, each player will have posted three antes to the pot, and the opening requirements will have advanced from jacks-or-better, to queens-or-better, to kings-or-better.

8.2.1 BLINDS, ANTES, AND BUTTONS

Because draw poker is a game of positional advantage, it is played with a dealer button that rotates around the table, thus affording every player the advantage of acting last (and the disadvantage of acting first).

In draw games played for high, antes are typically employed; in lowball, three blinds are used instead. Lowball blinds are placed by the players in the two seats immediately to the left of the dealer button, and the dealer posts a small blind on the button, for a total of three blind bets. Blinds can be used in draw played for high, too, although the standard version with antes is both more traditional and more popular.

The blinds are *live*, and if no one enters the pot for a raise, the blind has the option to raise her own bet.

8.2.2 DECKS AND DEALS

In all forms of draw poker as well as lowball, each player is dealt five cards face down. Draw games can and are played with a fifty-two-card deck, or a fifty-three-card deck that includes a joker or *bug* [see Rule 8.1].

Five cards are dealt to each player and the first round of betting begins. If jacks-or-better opening requirements are in place, any player opening the pot must have at least a pair of jacks, though once the pot has been opened other players may call or raise with any hand, without regard to whether or not they possess *openers*.

Once the first-round betting has equalized and concluded, players may replace any number of cards from their hand. This is called the *draw*, and anywhere from zero (playing a *pat hand*) to five cards may be passed to the dealer in exchange for an equal number of new cards. Many home games include variations on the number of cards allowed to be discarded/replaced, such as three, four-with-ace, and so on.

A second and final round of betting follows the discard and replacement process. Stakes double in limit games on the second round, much as they do on the turn in hold'em.

If more than one player remains after the final betting round concludes, a showdown determines the winner. Any player with more or fewer than five cards has a dead hand and is not eligible for the pot. If the game is *jacks-or-better,* the opener must be able to show that he began with a qualifying opening hand in order to win the pot. [For clarification, refer to Rules 8.2.10 and 8.2.11.]

Draw poker without a minimum opening requirement is usually referred to as either *California draw* or *guts*. In this version, players may open with any five cards, without regard to whether they have a pair of jacks or better.

8.2.3 ORDER OF PLAY

Whenever antes are used, action begins with the player to the immediate left of the dealer. If he cannot or opts not to open, that opportunity passes to the player on his left, and rotates in this fashion around the table. In games where there is an ante and blinds are not used, players have the option of passing—which is really a check (a bet of nothing)—on the opening round.

If no one opens, each player posts another ante and the opening requirement escalates to queens or better.

When blinds are used instead of antes, or if they are used in addition to antes, the first round's action commences with the player seated to the immediate left of the blinds. This player may fold, call, or raise the blind. When blinds are used in a high-only draw game, the jacks-or-better requirement is no longer operative, because the blind bet represents the opening bet and that player might not be holding openers.

After the draw, wagering begins with the player who opened the betting on the first round. Betting then proceeds clockwise around the table until the betting has been equalized or only one player remains active in the hand.

Whenever the opening player folds, action begins to the left of the opening position. When blinds are employed, action on the second round always commences with the player seated to the dealer's immediate left, if she is still active, and proceeds clockwise to the first active player in the event that the middle blind has folded.

On both the first and second rounds of betting, a bet and four raises are typically permitted, and check-raising is permitted both before and after the draw. If a betting round begins with only two players, there is no limit on the number of raises allowed.

8.2.4 *ASKING ABOUT NUMBER OF CARDS DRAWN*

You'll often hear this: "How many cards did you draw?" A player, or the dealer, is required to respond honestly if asked how many cards were drawn by another player. This requirement is only in effect until the first betting action following the draw. Once the first post-draw bet is made, the asked player is no longer obliged to answer and the dealer is forbidden to respond.

Similarly, after any betting round in any poker game, it is no longer acceptable for a player to ask, "who raised?" or for a dealer to respond. [See Rule 3.19.]

8.2.5 *PLAYER'S RIGHT TO CHANGE NUMBER OF CARDS DRAWN*

A player retains the right to change the number of cards that he wishes to draw, as long as the cards have not been dealt in response to the player's initial request, and no player has wagered or indicated the number of cards he wishes to draw, based on that initial request.

INTERPRETATION NOTE

You're free to change the number of cards you wish to draw, unless your initial request is followed by action from subsequent players or by the dealer. When that happens, the initial request is valid; any changes you may wish to make are not.

8.2.6 EXPOSED CARDS

Cards exposed by the dealer prior to the draw must be kept. Cards exposed by the dealer during the draw cannot be kept.

Exposed draw cards are replaced with new cards from the deck after all other players complete their draws.

8.2.7 RAPPING PAT

Rapping the table in turn during the first round indicates that a player is passing his option to open the pot. When done during the draw, rapping the table is a declaration of a *pat hand,* meaning that the player does not want to replace any of his cards.

8.2.8 GOING ALL-IN FOR ANTES

If a player opens the pot by going all-in for just the ante, or even for part of the ante, all callers must come in for the full opening bet. If a player is all-in for the antes but no one opens the pot and another ante is required, the all-in player may compete for the antes that he has matched. He will not be eligible to compete for a side pot comprising subsequently posted antes nor for any additional wagers.

If a player is all-in and declares the pot open without being able to show a qualifying hand, she loses her ante money and is not eligible to play on escalated rounds (queens-or-better, kings-or-better) until a winner is determined.

INTERPRETATION NOTE

Even if you buy in again, you still have to wait until that pot is concluded by a winner being declared until you are eligible to play. If you are all-in for either a partial or full ante, you may play for the antes or that portion of the antes covered by your partial ante. If another ante is required because no one opened the pot, you are eligible to compete for whatever part of the antes you were able to match.

8.2.9 JACKS-OR-BETTER, "SHOW OPENERS" REQUIREMENT

For the player who opens to win the pot in jacks-or-better, he must show his openers, even if no one else calls his opening bet.

8.2.10 OPENING WITH NON-QUALIFYING HANDS

Should the opening bettor show a hand prior to the replacement draw that is less than a pair of jacks (and therefore does not qualify to open the pot), any other player who has yet to act on his hand may open the pot.

This new opener will also have to prove he had a qualifying hand of jacks or better if he is to win the pot.

Any players who originally passed openers are not eligible to declare the pot open in this situation.

The player who opened with an unqualified hand has a dead hand, and is ineligible to continue on in the play of the hand. He also loses his opening bet, which stays in the pot. He may, however, withdraw any other bets he may have placed in the pot as long as the action before the draw has not concluded.

Any other bet placed in the pot by the opening bettor may be withdrawn, provided the action before the draw has not concluded.

If no other player declares the pot open, all bets are returned except the unqualified opener's first bet, which, along with her antes, remains in the pot. All players involved in the hand are entitled to play the next hand after anteing again, with the exception of the false opener.

INTERPRETATION NOTE

A player who declares the pot open becomes the new opener, even after a player who opens is disqualified because his hand did not meet the jacks-or-better threshold. The new opener must also prove he holds at least a pair of jacks to win the pot. If the opener cannot prove openers, or if the opening hand is fouled, all bets will be returned to participating players except for the opening bet and antes. Only those players who participated in a falsely opened hand may compete in the subsequent hand, and they must post an ante again.

However, if a raise has been made, two or more players call the opening bet, or all action is concluded before the draw, then the pot will play even if the opener shows or declares an unqualified hand.

Once the action before the draw is complete, the opener may not withdraw any bets he may have made, even if his hand fails to meet opening requirements. At the floor supervisor's discretion, a player opening the pot may be permitted to retrieve his hand to prove that his hand met the requirements to open the pot. Any player may request that the opener retain the opening hand and show it after the winner of the pot has been determined.

8.2.11 SPLITTING OPENERS

A player may open the pot, then decide to split his openers and discard one of them in order to draw a card or cards to improve his hand. To do this, he must announce that he is splitting openers and place his discards under a chip, so that they may be exposed by the dealer after the play of the hand concludes.

A player is ineligible to win the pot if he announces that he is splitting openers, but a subsequent comparison of his discards to his final hand proves he could not have held a qualifying hand at the time of his declaration.

8.3 JACKS BACK

Jacks back is a draw-poker game combining jacks-or-better draw poker with ace-to-five lowball. Cards are dealt to players as in draw poker, and jacks-or-better are required to open the pot. But if no player elects to open, or if no player has a qualifying opener, the game that began as high draw now morphs into lowball, and the player seated to the dealer's left is required to open the pot for the designated opening lowball bet.

INTERPRETATION NOTE

Splitting openers usually happens when a player has a two-way hand that can be played as a qualifying pair or as a draw to a straight or flush. If a player holds Q-Q-J-T-joker, he is eligible to open the betting with a pair of queens. But if he opens and an opponent raises, he might decide to split openers by discarding one of his two queens and drawing to a straight.

In this case he will announce that he is splitting openers, discard one of his queens by placing it under a chip where it can be retrieved when needed to verify that he did have a qualifying hand, and retain Q-J-T-joker in hopes of catching a king, ace, nine, or ace to complete his straight. By splitting openers a player is swapping a qualified opening hand for a draw to what promises to be a bigger hand if it is completed.

The keys to a player successfully splitting openers are twofold: first the player must announce that he is splitting openers. Then he must place any qualifying cards under a chip so that he can prove that he had qualifying openers if he is to win the pot.

This game is always played with antes, but a single blind bet is made by the player to the dealer's left when no one opens with jacks-or-better and the game becomes lowball. Any pot thus opened as lowball then follows all lowball rules. While check-raising is permitted when the pot is being contested for high, checking and raising is never permitted when the hand converts to lowball. Similarly, the *must-bet-sevens* rule [see Rule 8.5.4] applies when the hand switches to lowball format.

The opening-blind lowball bet is live and may be raised by the player making the forced bet if no one else raises before the action returns to him. In the event that the player to the left of the button has less than half the blind when the pot converts to lowball, the player to the blind's left must post a blind bet. If the all-in player wins the pot or buys in again, the button does not advance, so the all-in player is forced to post a full blind in the event that no one opens for high.

INTERPRETATION NOTE

Apply the high-only draw rules until the point at which the pot is unopened and the game converts to lowball. At that point, the single blind bet is posted (to the left of the dealer button) and all low-ball rules apply until the hand's conclusion.

8.4 LOWBALL

Lowball is a generic term for a related group of draw-poker games in which the lowest hand wins. The most common variety of the game is California lowball, which is also known as ace-to-five lowball. In this version, the best possible hand is 5-4-3-2-A, and straights and flushes do not count against you. In this version, aces are the lowest cards in the deck.

Another popular version is Kansas City lowball, also known as deuce-to-seven lowball. As you might expect from its name, the best hand in this lowball game is 7-6-5-4-2. In Kansas City lowball, aces are high cards only—they are never low—and straights and flushes count *against* you. In the strictest sense, Kansas City lowball represents the truest inversion of the hierarchy of poker hands detailed back in Rule 4.8, Hand Rankings.

8.5 CALIFORNIA LOWBALL

When people use the term "lowball" without further qualification, they're usually talking about California lowball (ace-to-five), which is the most popular lowball variant. The game is typically played with a joker or "bug" added to the deck as a fifty-third card, which plays as the lowest card not present in a player's hand. A bet and four raises are permitted.

INTERPRETATION NOTE

If you were dealt 7-6-4-2-joker, the joker would play like an ace, and your hand would be 7-6-4-2-A. If you were dealt 7-6-4-A-joker, the joker would play as a deuce—the lowest card NOT in your hand, and your hand would also be 7-6-4-2-A.

If you read your lowball hand from the highest card down to the lowest, always remember that an ace is low, not high, and that the joker is the lowest card not in your hand. This way you won't have any problem determining which low hand is best.

8.5.1 BLINDS, ANTES, AND BUTTONS

Although California lowball may be played with an ante, it is far more common for three players to each post a blind bet. Two blinds are typically posted to the dealer's left and a small blind is posted on the button. The button moves clockwise around the table at the conclusion of each deal, in turn providing all players the advantages and disadvantages of each playing position.

A player will receive a hand when it is his turn to post a blind, even if he has less than half a big blind. When this occurs the next player in turn must also post the big blind. The all-in player must post another big blind if he wins the pot or buys in again. If he prefers not to post after winning the pot, he shall be dealt out until it is again his turn to post the big blind. Half or more of the blind amount is considered to be a full blind for this procedure. A player winning the pot when posting at least half of the big blind will not have to post another big blind, as would be required if he had posted less than half of the big blind.

8.5.2 DECKS AND DEALS

Each player is dealt five cards face down, which is followed by a round of betting. Play begins with the person to the left of the blinds, and because the blinds are live wagers rather than antes, each player, acting in turn, must respond to the blind bets by electing to fold, call, or raise. Once betting has equalized and the initial betting round concludes, players have the opportunity to replace cards in their hands in hopes of improving it.

The rules governing the number of allowable bets and raises, as well as the rules for discarding, drawing, rapping pat, and responding to the question, "How many cards did you draw," are the same in lowball as in draw poker played for high.

Prior to the legalization of hold'em and stud games in California, when only draw and lowball games were legal in California, betting structures tended to vary by geography. In Southern California, lowball was played with betting limits that doubled after the draw. A typical game would be $6–$12 lowball, and the first round of betting featured increments of $6. After the draw, betting limits doubled and all wagering was in $12 units.

In Northern California, particularly in the San Francisco Bay area, betting limits were identical before and after the draw. A lowball game in the Bay Area would not be described as $6–$12, since that implied limits that doubled after the draw. Instead it was often described as *$6-straight,* and betting would be in six-dollar increments both before and after the draw.

8.5.3 DECLARING HANDS

Any verbal declaration by a player at the showdown is binding. A player who makes a declaration must be able to produce the hand he declared in order to win the pot. If a player's inaccurate declaration leads an opponent to throw his hand away, the player who incorrectly declared his hand is ineligible to win the pot.

If there are more than two players involved at the showdown, the incorrectly declared hand is dead and the best live hand wins the pot.

Players holding a pair in their hand are obliged to announce the pair's presence at the showdown. If they fail to announce a pair, and that failure causes an opponent to foul his hand, the player holding the pair in his hand may lose the pot. If two or more hands remain at the show-down, cards speak and the best hand wins the pot.

INTERPRETATION NOTE

If a player declares that he has a "seven-low" at the showdown, he'd better be able to produce at least a 7-6-5-4-3 to be eligible to win the pot. If not, his hand will be declared dead. If he declares a "smooth-seven" or "seven-a-b-c," he needs to produce 7-4-3-2-A to win the pot.

"Protect your hand at all times" is the best advice we can offer poker players. If a player declares a hand, make sure you see it and are sure it is a better hand than yours before folding.

8.5.4 BETTING SEVENS

In fixed-limit California lowball, any player who checks a seven-low or better and has the best hand after the draw is ineligible to win money wagered on subsequent bets, although she is eligible to win money committed to the pot before the draw.

This is called the *bet-sevens* or *must-bet-sevens* rule. If a bet of less than half the pot is made, a player holding a seven-low or better is permitted to call this bet after the draw and win. Should another player overcall a short bet and lose, the player who overcalled has his bet returned to him. If the player holding a seven-low or better completes the short bet to a full bet, all the wagering that follows will stand. Check-raising after the draw is not permitted in California lowball.

Whenever the game is played as a pot-limit or no-limit game, the *must-bet-sevens* rule does not apply—players may

INTERPRETATION NOTE

If you're playing California lowball and make a 7-6-4-3-2 after the draw, checking with the intention of raising is not an option available to you, as it would be in most other poker games. If you are first to act and have a seven-low or better, you must come out betting if you hope to win any of the money committed to the pot on this betting round.

If you believe that one of your opponents has a better hand than your seven-low, you may check, but if you do, you are ineligible to win any of the money wagered after the draw. If you check and your opponent bets a better hand than yours, he will win the entire pot, including your call after the draw. But if you check, he bets, and you call with the best hand, you can only win the money that was wagered prior to the draw.

In this instance, your opponent has a free shot at you. If he bets and you call after checking prior to his wager, he can win with the best hand. And if you check, then call his wager and win the pot, he will have his last bet returned to him because you did not "bet sevens."

check any hand after the draw without penalty—and check-raising is permissible at any time.

8.5.5 ENTERING THE GAME

A new player may wait for the big blind or kill the pot by doubling the amount of the big blind in order to receive a hand immediately.

ALTERNATE RULE: A new player may enter the game immediately (and kill the pot in doing so), only if no other players at the table object.

8.5.6 MISSING THE BLINDS

A player who misses her blind must wait until it is her turn to post the blind to receive a hand. In a lowball game with multiple blinds, a player may either wait for the big blind or kill the pot if the big blind has passed her seat.

ALTERNATE RULE: A player who missed the big blind may kill the pot as long as no active player objects. If there is an objection, the player who missed his big blind must wait until it is his turn to take the big blind.

This does not apply to seat changes. If a player has posted his blinds and changed seats, he will be dealt in when the relationship of his position to the blinds has been equalized, thereby entitling him to a hand.

8.5.7 EXPOSED CARDS

In limit California lowball, if the dealer accidentally exposes a card of seven or lower prior to the draw, that card must be accepted by the player. An exposed card higher than

> **INTERPRETATION NOTE**
>
> If a player moves in the direction of the blind, he is dealt in on the next hand. If he moves away from the blind, he must wait until the number of hands that pass him equates to the number of seats he moved away from the blind. If he moves two seats to his left—away from the blinds—he is required to miss the next two hands. This corresponds to the general rule on switching seats at the same table, covered in Rule 2.9.

seven is replaced after the deal has been completed. When an exposed card is replaced, it becomes the burn card.

A card that has been exposed may not be taken after the draw. Instead, each player completes his or her draw and then the exposed card is replaced.

Any card flashed before the draw is not treated as an exposed card unless it lands face up without any intervention on the part of the player. After the draw, all flashed cards are considered exposed cards and replaced.

In pot-limit and no-limit lowball, a player must accept an exposed wheel card—one of 5-4-3-2-A—before the draw. Any other card must be replaced.

Exposed cards of any rank are replaced after the draw.

8.6 KANSAS CITY LOWBALL

Kansas City lowball, which is also called *deuce-to-seven lowball*, is played with a fifty-two-card deck. The best hand in this game is 7-5-4-3-2, as long as those cards are not of the same suit. Flushes, as with straights, or the rarer straight flushes, count against you in this game; a seemingly low hand that is a straight or a flush is not much of a low hand at all. Also, aces are *not* low cards in this game; they play as high cards only.

Any exposed card of 7, 5, 4, trey, or deuce must be accepted by the receiving player in Kansas City lowball.

INTERPRETATION NOTE

A clarification of the classic "wheel" hand, 5-4-3-2-A, illustrates one of the major hand-ranking differences between California (ace-to-five) and Kansas City (deuce-to-seven) lowball. In California, the 5-4-3-2-A is the immortal nuts, the best hand possible.

In Kansas City, 5-4-3-2-A is neither a straight—since aces are not low cards as well as high cards, as they are in other forms of poker—nor is it a very good low hand. Instead of being read 5-4-3-2-A, it is read as A-5-4-3-2. While this hand beats all other ace-high hands, it will lose to any king-high hand or lower that has no paired cards and is not a straight or flush.

By the same measure, any hand that would be a six-low in California lowball would either be a straight if it did not contain an ace, or an ace-low in deuce-to-seven lowball. Try as you might, the best hand you can make in Kansas City is neither a wheel nor a six-low. It's 7-5-4-3-2.

Any other card that's exposed must be replaced, and this *includes a six*. Exposed cards of any rank must be replaced after the draw.

Check-raising is permissible in deuce-to-seven and there is no requirement to bet sevens. All other draw and lowball rules not countermanded by rules in this section apply to Kansas City lowball.

8.7 DEUCE-TO-SEVEN TRIPLE DRAW

Deuce-to-seven lowball may also be played as a triple-draw game, and it is played with a maximum of six players. Traditional lowball games have two rounds of betting and one opportunity to draw in order to replace cards and make a better hand, but four rounds of betting and three draws are the hallmarks of this game.

8.7.1 BLINDS AND BUTTONS

A dealer button is used to indicate the order of betting and drawing. The player to the dealer's immediate left posts a small blind and the player to his immediate left posts a big blind. Both blinds are live.

8.7.2 DISCARDS AND DRAWS

After each round of betting players may discard up to five cards and draw replacements in order to improve their hand. A round of betting follows each draw, and one final betting round takes place after the third replacement opportunity has concluded.

8.7.3 WAGERING ROUNDS

Just as in Texas hold'em, the initial betting round begins with the player to the left of the big blind. That player may fold, call, or raise. If he folds, those options move to the folded player's left, and so on around the table.

After the first round is complete and the betting has been equalized, each active player may draw cards. Players act in turn and discard any cards they wish to replace, or stand pat. The player who is seated to the left of the button acts first in each discard-replacement sequence.

INTERPRETATION NOTE

The dealer gathers each player's discards in turn and brings them to the muck after dealing him his replacement cards. If Larry draws three cards, Moe draws two, and Curly stands pat, the dealer pitches Larry three cards and gathers his discards into the muck. Then he pitches two cards to Moe and gathers in his discards. Since Curly raps the table and announces he is standing pat, the replacement round is complete and players may wager again.

In triple draw, players have three opportunities to draw replacement cards for their hands before the final round of wagering takes place.

8.7.4 INSUFFICIENT CARDS

If too few cards are available to complete a drawing round, the muck is shuffled and used to complete the draw. The universe of cards available to complete the draw therefore includes discards from previous drawing rounds and discards from any player who received all of his replacement cards on the current round.

8.7.5 BETTING LIMITS

Fixed-limit triple-draw games use the same betting structure found in Texas hold'em, with the first two rounds at the lower limit and the last two rounds at the higher limit, normally double that of the earlier rounds.

> **INTERPRETATION NOTE**
>
> If you were playing $10–$20 limit triple-draw deuce-to-seven lowball, wagers would be made in increments of $10 on the first two rounds and $20 on the final two rounds.

8.8 ACE-TO-FIVE TRIPLE DRAW

This game plays identically to deuce-to-seven triple draw except for the fact that hands rank differently. In this variant of triple draw, hands are ranked as they are in ace-to-five lowball. Straights and flushes do not count against you. An ace is a low card and the best possible hand is 5-4-3-2-A.

All of the rules and procedures for this game are identical to those of deuce-to-seven, with the exception of hand rankings.

PART FOUR

Tournaments

CHAPTER 9

TOURNAMENT RULES

Tournaments differ dramatically from cash games, and while the versions of poker that are played are identical to those played outside of a tournament area, there are a variety of special tournament rules. The Tournament Directors Association, a voluntary and informal aggregation of tournament directors, poker managers, casino and card room executives, and others concerned with working toward a uniform set of rules and procedures for tournament poker, developed a set of uniform rules called the TDA rules.

Your authors wish to thank the TDA for permission to reproduce their rules in our book. Each rule in this section that contains an asterisk* next to it is excerpted directly from the TDA rules, with only minor changes where necessary to provide clarity of wording.

Where no asterisk is present, the authors have either added a rule that was not included in the TDA rules, veered toward an alternate ruling, or rewritten the TDA rule to the extent that it can no longer be considered a verbatim copy.

9.1 TOURNAMENT RULES AND PROCEDURES

Players who enter tournaments are bound to abide by both the tournament rules and the canons of etiquette that are administered by the tournament director and floor supervisors. Violators may be warned, suspended from play for a specified length of time, or disqualified from the tournament. Chips belonging to a disqualified player will be removed from play.

9.2 A BASIS FOR FAIR DECISION MAKING*

Floor people are to consider the best interests of the game and fairness as the top priority in the decision-making process. Unusual circumstances can, on occasion, dictate that the technical interpretation of the rules be ignored in the interest of fairness. The floor person's decision is final.

INTERPRETATION NOTE

The traditions of poker, game fairness, and the best interests of the game will overrule a narrower, doctrinaire approach to rule enforcement. Where there is an apparent conflict between the letter of the rule and the spirit of the game, the spirit and traditions of poker shall prevail.

9.3 CASH GAME RULES

Whenever possible, all rules are the same as those that apply to live games.

9.4 STARTING CHIPS AND SEATED PLAYERS

Starting chips will be placed in front of the seat of each player who has paid an entry fee. This will be done even if the player is not present. Each stack of chips at the table will be dealt a hand regardless of whether a player is present or absent for a hand or series of hands. Antes and blinds will be taken from all players who have entered the tournament—whether they are present for a hand or not. Hands will be mucked of players who are not seated by the time the deal is complete. Once the cards are dealt, the dealer will muck unseated player's hands before beginning the action.

ALTERNATE RULE: The player's cards will be mucked if he hasn't been seated by the time the action gets to him.

9.5 NO CHIP TRANSFERS PERMITTED

Chips may never be transferred from one player to another, and the tournament director will expel from the tournament players caught transferring chips.

9.6 CHIPS IN FULL VIEW

Players have an absolute right to know how much money each opponent has in play, and all money in play shall be in full view at all times. In pot-limit and no-limit tournaments, large-denomination chips should be stacked in front so they are not hidden from view by a player's lower denomination chips. Before acting in pot-limit or no-limit tournaments, a player may ask the dealer to *count down* his opponents' chips.

9.7 NO-SHOW PLAYERS

Chips from players who paid an entry fee but fail to show up for the tournament will be removed from play after a period of time. The decision to collect the chips of absent players, thereby eliminating them from tournament contention, is at the discretion of the tournament director, providing that all players who are no-shows will be declared eliminated from the tournament simultaneously.

INTERPRETATION NOTE

Picking up chips from no-show players is usually done following the commencement of a new betting level, or after an hour has elapsed, whichever occurs first.

9.8 LATE ENTRANTS

A starting stack of chips may be placed in front of any vacant seat to accommodate late entrants. While that seat remains unsold, all antes and blinds will be paid. Unsold seats will be closed and chips in front of those seats will be picked up no later than the tournament director's declaration that chips from absent entrants are to be collected.

9.9 REMOVING LOWER DENOMINATION CHIPS*

When it is time to color-up chips, they will be raced off with a maximum of one chip going to any player. The chip race will always start in the No. 1 seat. A player cannot be

INTERPRETATION NOTE

If Joe is late getting to an event but some unsold seats still remain available, he may enter. However, he will not receive a full stack of chips because the chips in front of the seat he will occupy have hand blinds or antes taken from them just as if the seat were occupied by a player who had been there since the tournament's inception.

raced out of a tournament. In the event that a player has only one chip left, the regular race procedure will take place. If that player loses the race, he will be given one chip of the smallest denomination still in play.

INTERPRETATION NOTE

Chips will be removed from play when the lowest denomination chip still in play is no longer needed for wagering, or for the blind or ante structure. As part of this procedure, each player receives an equivalent whole number of higher denomination chips for those chips in his possession that are to be removed from play. When it is time to color-up chips, they will be raced-off to the highest card or cards. Two governing principles of coloring up are:

✓ No player will receive more than one new chip.
✓ No player will be raced out of a tournament.

If a player has too few chips in total to exchange at full value for one new chip, the regular race procedure will take place. If that player loses the race, he will be given one chip of the smallest denomination still in play.

When it's time to remove the five-dollar chips from play and exchange them for twenty-five-dollar chips, here's an example of what might happen: Deirdre, who has fifteen five-dollar chips in her possession will exchange them for three twenty-five-dollar chips. Since she was not left with any odd chips, she will not take part in the race and receives a dollar-for-dollar exchange on her chips.

Philip has seventeen five-dollar chips in his hand and exchanges fifteen of them for three twenty-five-dollar chips. The two remaining five-dollar chips are placed in front of him for the race.

Scott has only two five-dollar chips in his possession. He will race them off and if he is one of the race winners, he will be given a twenty-five-dollar chip. If he loses the race, he will still be given a twenty-five-dollar chip since no player may be eliminated from a tournament by virtue of a chip race.

Michael has only one odd chip remaining after exchanging his five-dollar chips. Quinn has four odd chips remaining after swapping his five-dollar chips.

Cards are then dealt so that each player in the race receives one card for each odd chip. Philip, with two chips, gets two cards and is dealt the ace of spades and the king of hearts.

Scott, with two chips also receives two cards: the nine of hearts and the deuce of clubs.

Michael receives the queen of diamonds.

Quinn receives four cards: the queen of clubs, jack of diamonds, four of spades, and four of hearts.

There are nine odd chips in this race, and two new chips will be awarded. Philip, who was dealt the two highest cards, is awarded only one chip, since no player may win more than one new chip in a race.

Michael, who holds the queen of diamonds, has the next highest card once those in Philip's hand have been accounted for. He would normally win the second chip. But not in this case.

Scott, who is short-stacked with a total of only four five-dollar chips in his possession, will be given the second and last odd chip since he cannot be eliminated from a tournament by virtue of losing a chip race—which is what would have occurred if that rule were not in place.

9.10 SPLITTING THE POT AMONG TIED HANDS*

The odd chip(s) will go to the high hand. In flop games, when there are two or more high hands or two or more low hands, the odd chip(s) will go to the left of the button. In stud-type games, the odd chip will go to the high card by suit. There will be an exception to this rule: an attempt will be made in identical hand situations to split the pot as evenly as possible: example—a wheel in Omaha/8.

ALTERNATE RULE: No player will be awarded two odd chips from the same pot.

INTERPRETATION NOTE

If two or more hands are identical, they tie and the pot is split among those players. Any odd chip should be broken down to the smallest denomination used in that game. Whenever two or more hands tie, an odd chip will be awarded to the first hand to the left (clockwise) of the button in flop games such as hold'em or Omaha.

In stud games the odd chip should be awarded to the high card by suit in high stud games, and to the low card by suit in low stud games such as razz, and to the high hand in high-low split games. All side pots as well as the main pot should be split as though they were separate pots, and will not be mixed together before they are split.

❋❋❋❋❋❋❋❋❋❋❋

This amusing anecdote is courtesy of Matt Lessinger.

TOPIC
Multicultural Miscommunications: The Case of the Extra Chip

I was playing $15–$30 hold'em, and a completely novice player sat down at the table. He was looking for some help from the dealer, but unfortunately the dealer was Asian and hardly spoke any English, and the English he did speak was thickly accented. So the other players did the best they

could to intervene and get the newbie started. For instance, he had sat down right in the big blind, so they explained to him that he had to post three five-dollar chips. Of course, he took one look at his cards and folded even though there was no pre-flop raise, so clearly he needed some help.

Two hands later, he called from the button in a multi-way pot. On the river, the board was K-Q-J-10-6 with no flush possible, so any ace was the nuts. Someone in early position bet, the action was folded to our friend on the button, and he merely called and showed his A-6 offsuit. The bettor showed A-J to claim half the pot, muttering about how he wasn't expecting the button to have an ace since he didn't raise.

Anyhow, the dealer begins splitting the pot and finds that there is an extra odd chip. He makes a bigger-than-necessary show of giving the odd chip to the early position player, while saying out loud "closest to the button."

The newbie then becomes genuinely puzzled, "Why does he get the extra chip?"

"Closest to the button," says the Asian dealer, a man of few English words.

"But he's not. I am," says the newbie.

"No, no, he is closer to button," says the dealer.

The newbie, who up until that point had been quite mild mannered, suddenly became very angry. He stood up, grabbed the dealer button off the table, and glaring right at the dealer, he said, "How can he be closest to the damn button?? It's right in front of me!!" Really it was quite amusing, but I *knew the man was genuinely becoming confused and flustered, so I did my best not to laugh.*

At that point the floorman finally came over and intervened, calmly explaining to the button that the rule gives the extra chip to the person in earlier position. The player then wanted to know why the dealer kept saying it was the person "closest to the button" who got the odd chip. The floorman said that was just the way it was phrased, and really it is not a good way of putting it.

The players at the table then pondered why anyone had ever started saying that the odd chip goes to the player "closest to the button," when in reality the person actually sitting closest to the button (i.e., the button himself) can never get the odd chip. The odd chip goes to the player "in earliest position," and we all agreed that is how it should be phrased in every card room.

9.11 SIDE POTS*

Each side pot will be split as a separate pot. They will not be mixed together before they are split.

9.12 TIME LIMITS FOR ACTING ON A HAND*

Once a reasonable amount of time has passed and a clock is called for, a player will be given one minute to make a decision. If action has not been taken by the time the minute is over, there will be a ten-second countdown. If a player has not acted on her hand by the time the countdown is over, the hand will be dead.

INTERPRETATION NOTE

The rule is the same in tournaments and in cash games. A player is required to act on her hand in a reasonable amount of time. If the time seems overly long, any player is free to request that the player in question be "put on the clock." That player is given one minute to act. If she does not act, the floor supervisor or tournament director begins a ten-second countdown. If the player has not acted when the countdown reaches zero, her hand is dead.

9.13 DEAD BUTTON RULE*

Tournament play will use a dead button.

9.14 EXPOSING CARDS WITH ACTION PENDING*

A penalty *may* be invoked if a player exposes any card with action pending, if a card goes off the table, if soft-play occurs, or similar incidents take place. Penalties *will* be invoked in cases of abuse, disruptive behavior, or similar incidents.

INTERPRETATION NOTE

Two major variations for blind rules are prevalent: the "forward moving button" and the "dead button." When a dead button is used, a player can be in the dealer position more than once a round, but there'll always be one big and one small blind per hand.

Under forward moving button procedures, the button always advances, even if someone gets up and leaves in the midst of his or her blinds. When this happens it is sometimes necessary to have two big blinds and one small blind, or two small blinds and one big blind in the same hand to equalize the blinds with the forward-moving button.

In the interest of uniformity we recommend standardizing on the dead button procedure in tournaments and cash games alike.

9.15 PLAYERS MUST BE AT THE TABLE TO CALL TIME*

A player must be at the table by the time all players have complete hands in order to have his hand considered to be live. Players must be at the table to call time.

INTERPRETATION NOTE

The tournament director or one of his assistants, not the dealer, always makes penalty calls. The dealer is responsible for conveying the facts and circumstances to the tournament director or floor supervisor, who will also gather input when required from players, and render a decision consistent with past practices and precedent in that tournament.

INTERPRETATION NOTE

In a tournament, you can't call "time" as you're walking back to your seat in order to have the action stop so you can look at your hand. If you're not in your seat by the time the last card has been pitched to the last player in the dealing order, you are deemed to be absent from the table, and your hand will be folded.

9.16 FACE UP WHEN ALL-IN AND ALL ACTION IS COMPLETE*

All cards will be turned face up once a player is all-in and all action is complete.

INTERPRETATION NOTE

This has become standard operating procedure for tournaments during the past few years. Once one or more players are all-in and no side pot is possible, then all players in the hand must turn their hands face up.

9.17 FIFTY PERCENT RULE FOR RAISING·

If a player puts in a raise of 50 percent or more of the previous bet, he will be required to make a full raise. The raise will be exactly the minimum raise allowed.

INTERPRETATION NOTE

If a player fails to say "raise," and announces that the bet is a particular amount that is 50 percent or more than the previous bet but less than the correct raise, that player shall be held to the minimum raise.

9.18 OVERSIZED CHIPS*

In limit games, an oversized chip will be constituted to be a call if the player does not announce a raise. In no-limit, an oversized chip before the flop is a call; after the flop, an oversized chip put in the pot by the initial bettor will constitute the size of the bet. In pot-limit and no-limit, if a player states "raise" and throws in an oversized chip, the raise will be the maximum amount allowable up to the size of that chip.

INTERPRETATION NOTE

When raising in a no-limit or pot-limit tournament, a player must either put the amount of the raise out in one motion, or state the amount of the raise. By stating the word "raise," a player protects his right to raise, but the raise must be made in one additional motion unless he states the amount.

The oversized chip bet is a major poker argument provoker. As a player, the best way to reserve your right to raise is to say, "Raise," when it's your turn to act. Once you announce your intention to raise, you can go back and put chips in the pot. But if you don't announce the amount of your raise, you'll be limited to the number of chips you put in the pot with the first motion.

It's also confusing when a player says something like, "Raise, twenty dollars." Suppose there's ten dollars in the pot. Does "Raise, twenty dollars" mean the raiser is adding another twenty dollars to the pot, making the new total thirty dollars? Or is he raising the pot so that it totals twenty dollars, which he plans to accomplish by adding another ten dollars to it?

The easiest way to accomplish this without causing confusion is to announce the new size of the pot once your raise has been made. If there's a ten-dollar pot and you'd like to add twenty dollars to that total, you can make things crystal clear by saying, "Raise, thirty dollars to go," or "Raise, play for thirty," or "The bet is thirty dollars straight." Train yourself to do this, and you can be certain your action will never be misconstrued and you won't be the cause of any altercations at the poker table.

9.19 ONE PLAYER PER HAND*

The one-player-to-a-hand rule will be enforced.

9.20 RANDOM SEAT ASSIGNMENTS*

Tournament and satellite seats will be randomly assigned.

INTERPRETATION NOTE

This particular problem occurs frequently in stud games, because some players have difficulty seeing from one end of the table all the way to the other end. Assigning the middle seats last can easily rectify it, thereby reserving middle seats for players who are visually handicapped. While not a strictly random procedure, it does strike a balance between pure randomization and accommodating players who might otherwise be at a severe disadvantage.

Similarly, we recommend accommodating players in wheelchairs in end seats, because it is frequently difficult for players in wheelchairs to move into middle seats. While we favor random seating, we also recommend diverging from a strictly randomized seating practice in order to accommodate players with special needs.

ALTERNATE RULE: Tournament and satellite seats will be randomly assigned, however, seats directly across from the dealer, which are the No. 5 seat at a nine-handed table, or the No. 4 and No. 5 seats at an eight-handed table, or the No. 5 and No. 6 seats at a ten-handed table, will be assigned last and reserved for players who have difficulty seeing from one of the end seats.

9.21 ENGLISH-ONLY RULE*

The English-only rule will be enforced in the United States during the play of hands.

INTERPRETATION NOTE

In non-English-speaking countries, the local language or languages will be used during the play of the hands. If English is also a commonly spoken language, local rules and customs may dictate that English is allowable in addition to local languages.

Dave Lamb reports this story.

TOPIC
Cultural Differences: The Case of the Kibbitzers

A common rule in poker is that talking to players during a hand is prohibited. Nevertheless, in some *cultures, poker is much more a social occasion than it is in others. For example, there were five live players in a $50/$100 Omaha game at the Taleon Club, in St. Peterburg, Russia. Yet, there were thirteen people seated around the table—eating, drinking, and visiting with players and each other.*

Lesson

Clearly, one had to recognize that the cultural dynamics here were considerably different from what may be customary in the United States or elsewhere. First and foremost, this was not a public casino, but a "club," in which a greater degree of familiarity and comfort was permitted. Furthermore, for Russians and Eastern Europeans, gambling, particularly poker, was more a social occasion than it might be for American or Western European poker players.

Gaming and competition, gambling and betting behaviors are often culturally determined. Consequently, despite well-intentioned rules and protocol, and while our purpose is to assure a professional, fair event, cultural respect and sensitivity requires flexibility and adaptability. Therefore, it's important to invest some time and effort to acquire a cultural awareness, as well as knowledge of local customs and card club rules.

9.22 MOBILE PHONE USE AT THE TABLE*

A player who wants to use a cellular phone must step away from the table.

> **INTERPRETATION NOTE**
>
> A player talking at the table on a mobile phone will be treated as though he is away from the table. Cards will be dealt to his position, but will be swept away when the action reaches him. If the player looks at his hand while on a mobile call, his hand will be deemed to have been fouled.

9.23 FOREIGN CHIPS*

There will be no foreign chips on the table except for a maximum of one card cap.

9.24 DECK CHANGES*

Deck changes will be on the dealer push or limit changes or as prescribed by the house. Players may not ask for deck changes.

9.25 WHEN NEW BETTING LIMITS APPLY*

When time has elapsed in a round and a new round is announced, the new limits apply to the next hand. A new hand begins with the first riffle.

INTERPRETATION NOTE

The tournament rule differs from rules employed in cash games, and the reason is that deck changes take time. In order to ensure that all players have the same amount of effective time in which to play hands at each wagering limit, deck changes will not be made except as specified above.

9.26 PLAYER MAY NOT MISS A HAND*

A player may not miss a hand. If a player announces the intent to re-buy before the first card is dealt, that player is playing behind and is obligated to make the re-buy.

INTERPRETATION NOTE

A player without chips must specify the amount he is playing behind, then produce that sum of money in order to be dealt a hand. When someone is playing behind, chips equivalent to his action shall be pulled from the pot and placed in front of him each time he bets, calls, or raises. This will provide a correct accounting of the money he owes the winner of the pot.

9.27 KEEPING CHIPS VISIBLE*

Players must keep their highest denomination chips visible at all times.

9.28 ALL CHIPS MUST BE VISIBLE*

All chips must be visibly displayed at all times. Players may not have tournament chips in their pockets at any time. A player who has chips in his pocket will forfeit the chips. The forfeited chips will be taken out of play from the tournament.

INTERPRETATION NOTE

Players have an absolute right to know how much money every other player at the table has in play. All money in play shall be kept in full view. In pot-limit and no-limit cash games and tournaments, large-denomination chips should be stacked in front so they are not hidden from view or otherwise obscured by a player's lower denomination chips.

Before acting in pot-limit or no-limit games, a player has the right to ask the dealer to "count down" his opponents' chips.

Because a tournament is time-sensitive by its nature, the dealer should not count down an all-in player's chips unless asked for a count by one of the players in the hand.

9.29 VERBAL DECLARATION REGARDING HAND CONTENT*

Verbal declarations as to the content of a player's hand are not binding; however, at management's discretion, any player deliberately miscalling his hand may be penalized.

9.30 RABBIT HUNTING*

No rabbit hunting is allowed.

INTERPRETATION NOTE

Rabbit hunting is the term given to searching through the remainder of the deck to see what you would have made if you had stayed in the pot. It slows down the game as well as provides additional information to players about cards that remain in the deck, and by implication, cards that must be in an opponent's hand.

Rabbit hunting is not allowed in most cash games, either, and even in those casinos with no rule expressly prohibiting rabbit hunting, it is frowned upon and considered a breach of poker etiquette.

9.31 BLIND DODGING*

A player who intentionally dodges a blind when moving from a broken table will forfeit the blind he should have posted and may incur a penalty. The money will be put into the next pot and is considered dead money.

INTERPRETATION NOTE

The tournament director or one of his floor supervisors, not the dealer, will make the imposition of a penalty. The decision will be based on facts and circumstances, along with past practices established at the casino and tournament.

9.32 MOVING PLAYERS*

In flop games, players will be moved from the big blind to the worst position.

INTERPRETATION NOTE

The intent of this practice is to put a player who has moved into a position at the new table most like the one he vacated at his old one. If a player can be moved into the big blind, he will. If the big blind seat is not vacant, he will be moved into whichever vacant seat is nearest to the big blind's left.

9.33 NUMBER OF RAISES IN LIMIT EVENTS*

In limit events, there will be a limit to raises, even when heads-up. The limit will be the house limit. Once the tournament becomes head-up the rule does not apply.

9.34 EXPOSED DOWN CARDS IN STUD GAMES*

In stud-type games, if any of the players' two down cards are exposed due to dealer error, it is a misdeal.

INTERPRETATION NOTE

This rule differs from cash game stud rules, in which an exposed card will remain with the player and the card that would have been his exposed card will be dealt face down.

9.35 KILLING UNPROTECTED HANDS*

If a dealer kills an unprotected hand, the player will have no redress and will not be entitled to his money back. However, if a player raises and his raise has not been called yet, he is entitled to receive his raise back.

9.36 CARDS SPEAK*

A dealer may not kill a winning hand that was turned face up and was obviously the winning hand.

9.37 VERBAL DECLARATIONS MADE IN TURN*

A verbal declaration of "fold," "call," "raise," or "re-raise" made in turn is binding. Action out of turn *may* be binding. [See Rule 3.18.]

INTERPRETATION NOTE

If a dealer kills the winning hand in error, that hand may be reconstructed if it can be retrieved from the muck intact, or if it can be reconstructed by reviewing surveillance tapes. The goal of this rule is to ensure that the best hand wins and that dealer error should not result in a lesser hand being awarded the pot.

ALTERNATE RULE: Money placed in the betting circle out of turn shall remain in the pot, even if a player decides to fold. A player who bets out of turn will be held to that bet if all players who are to act before him fold or check.

ALTERNATE RULE: A player who checks out of turn will only be allowed to call, check, or fold when the action gets to him.

INTERPRETATION NOTE

The tournament director or one of his assistants, not the dealer, will make this decision. The dealer is responsible for conveying the facts and circumstances to the tournament director or floor supervisor, who will also gather input when required from players, and render a decision consistent with past practices and precedent in that tournament.

❈❈❈❈❈❈❈❈❈❈❈❈

This story is from WSOP (World Series of Poker) tournament director Matt Savage.

TOPIC
Verbal Declaration: The Case of the Careless Fold.

This fiasco happened at the main event of the World Series of Poker and has been shown in televised reruns on countless occasions; it's become part of poker history. Russ Rosenblum opened the pot for a raise only to find himself called by British pro Julian Gardner, who was on the button. Rosenblum came out betting $18,000 into a T-T-3 flop. But Julian Gardner raised, making it $50,000 to go. Russ had a good long think, then said, "Let's play for a hundred."

Gardner said, "All in!" and in one motion brought his chips forward with two hands. Julian had a lot of chips, but they were mostly of small denomination, rendering them great in number but rather small in value. Rosenblum jumped up and leaned against a wall, a good eight feet from the table.

Matt Savage continues:

That's when I stepped up to the table and stood behind the dealer, asking him, "Where's Russell?" I located Russell against the wall and heard the player weakly declare with a wave of his arm, "I fold. Fold."

Then, almost as an afterthought, Rosenblum asked, "How much is the raise?" He came alive again in an instant, rushed back to the table, and grabbed for his cards. But I was faster, and my hand was there, too, clamping a vise on Russell's out-stretched wrist. In a firm and calm voice I said, "I'm sorry, Russell. You've folded. Verbal action in turn is compulsory."

Assessment

Savage not only made the correct decision, he made it without being called to the table. Matt Savage acted appropriately and rendered the correct decision. To his credit, even Russ Rosenblum agreed.

9.38 MOVING FROM A BROKEN TABLE*

A player who is moved from a broken table to a new seat at another table assumes the rights and responsibilities of the position he is assigned at the new table. A player may be seated in the big blind, the small blind, or on the button. The only place a player may not be dealt a hand is between the small blind and the button. Any player who is moved to balance tables will take the worst position. A dead button situation may occur.

9.39 PENALTIES FOR INFRACTIONS*

Penalties available for use by the tournament director are verbal warnings or time away from the table. A penalty of ten-, twenty-, thirty-, and forty minutes away from the table, as well as disqualification, may be invoked at the tournament director's or floor supervisor's discretion. Any player who is disqualified will have his chips removed from play. Blinds and antes shall be taken from players serving a penalty of time away from the table.

INTERPRETATION NOTE

If you are penalized, it will cost you. Not only in terms of lost opportunities, but you will be dealt hands you are unable to play. As a result, blinds and antes shall be taken from your stack during a penalty. A player serving a penalty may be blinded out of the tournament.

9.40 NO PLAYER SHALL DISCUSS A HAND IN PLAY*

No player, whether in the hand or not, shall discuss a hand until the action is complete. By playing in a tournament, each participant assumes an obligation to protect other competitors at all times. A penalty may be given for discussion of hands during the play. It is forbidden to discuss cards that have been discarded or hand possibilities, and doing so is subject to penalty.

9.41 EXPOSING A CARD WHILE A HAND IS IN PLAY*

A player who exposes his cards during the play may incur a penalty, but will not have his hand killed.

INTERPRETATION NOTE

Discussing a hand in play, or speculating aloud on possible hands, provides information to other players and violates the one player per hand rule.

ALTERNATE RULE: Repeatedly exposing cards will result in additional penalties, including expulsion from the tournament, at the discretion of the floor.

INTERPRETATION NOTE

Exposing cards during the play of a hand provides additional information to players and violates the one player per hand rule.

9.42 ONE MOTION*

In no-limit or pot-limit, when raising, a player must either put the amount of the raise out in one motion or state the raise amount. By stating the word *raise*, a player protects his right to raise, but the raise must be made in one additional motion unless he states the amount.

9.43 VERBALLY DISCLOSING THE CONTENTS OF A HAND*

Verbally disclosing the contents of your hand or advising a player how to play a hand may result in a penalty.

Sheree Bykofsky relates this tale from a casino tournament.

TOPIC
Talking: The Case of the Chatty All-In

Sheree was one of three players left in a one-table satellite tournament at a well-known casino. Sheree folded her hand on the button. One player, who had been bluffing frequently, raised all-in and tried to convince the other player to fold by saying, "I'm not on a draw this time." In other words, he was stating that he had at least a pair. Sheree was out of the hand, but if one of the players were to be knocked out, she would have benefited, and so she called over the floor to see if talking about one's hand—even obliquely—was permissible. The tournament floor supervisor came over to the table and the question was posed. The floor supervisor said that anyone can say anything about his hand. Sheree asked a question to clarify, "Do you mean that this player could have said, 'I flopped a set of nines'?" "Yes," said the floor supervisor as she walked away. Sheree felt this was unfair and later found the casino's tournament rules. The fifth rule clearly showed that the floor supervisor had ruled in error: "The one player to a hand rule will be enforced. Players may not make verbal statements as to the contents of their hand. Players doing so will be warned or penalized."

Assessment

The rule makes sense. To allow players to talk about their hands during tournaments can easily lead to collusion and unfair treatment to players.

9.44 LESS THAN A FULL RAISE*

In no-limit and pot-limit, less than a full raise does not reopen the betting to a player who already has acted.

9.45 CHOPPING BLINDS

Chopping blinds shall not be permitted in tournaments. [See Rule 2.39.]

9.46 RE-BUY TOURNAMENTS

Some tournaments allow players to re-buy and/or add-on chips at or before a certain time period has passed and based on the number of chips a player possesses before re-buy or add-on. Some re-buy tournaments require that players play at least one hand before re-buying or diminish their stack before re-buying. Other re-buy tournaments allow players to re-buy before the first hand is dealt. It may be important to know all of the individual house re-buy rules before sitting down to play in a re-buy tournament. Two rules common to all re-buy tournaments are:

✓ A player must verbally request a re-buy before the cards are dealt and the dealer should acknowledge request. This re-buy request is binding.

✓ A player may not miss a hand after losing all of his chips. He must either re-buy before the next hand or leave the tournament.

****

The following story was submitted by Sheree Bykofsky.

TOPIC

Show One, Show All: The Case of the Non-Verbal Re-Buy and the Biased Dealer and Table

After winning the woman's event at a well-known Vegas casino, I registered for a $200 re-buy event. My table was filled with men, some of whom had clearly not played before. I asked the dealer if I needed to play a hand before re-buying and he wasn't sure but found out that I could re-buy before the first hand. I called for a re-buy. I was aware that I was the only one at the table who had verbally called for a re-buy. Others started taking cash out of their pocket. The re-buy man came over and asked the man in the No. 7 seat if he wished a re-buy. He began doling out chips to re-buyers one player at a time starting with the No. 7 seat and going counter-clockwise around the table. He gave me my re-buy and was going around the table to see who else wanted a re-buy.

In the meantime, I was in the hand. I decided to go all-in against a player in the No. 1 seat who had not yet done a re-buy or asked for one, knowing that I only had to cover the original bet. He called my bet. Then I said, before the cards were turned over, "I'm confirming that he hasn't done his re-buy yet."

The dealer said, as he made us turn over the cards and saw that my opponent had flopped a set, "He has cash in front of him. That constitutes a re-buy."

I said, "Did you hear him ask for a re-buy?" The dealer said it didn't matter, he had money in front of him. A man next to the dealer said he had heard the No. 1 seat (who didn't seem to have ever played in a tournament before) ask for a re-buy (he hadn't because he didn't know he needed to!!!).

The people fighting for the man's right to a re-buy did not realize it was important for the man to have verbalized his request. He did not verbalize it!

The chip runner who was doling out the re-buys confirmed that he had not heard the man ask for a re-buy as did two other players at the table who knew the rules. The floor was called over and by that time, the dealer realized he had to answer the floor's question about whether the man had called for a re-buy with a "yes." He was just waiting his turn as all of the men with cash on the table were doing. But he was the only one in the hand. The floor said he had to stand by his dealer. And that was that. $400 dollars. I was finished in one hand. I would not have gone all-in if I had to do it with my buy-in and re-buy.

Sheree's Assessment

The man doling out the re-buys should not have been doling them out counterclockwise at the table. He should have started with the first person who requested a re-buy—Sheree—and then continued to players who said they wanted a re-buy or to the players that the dealer identified as having verbally requested a re-buy. The dealer should not have said that it didn't matter if a player had requested a re-buy, that the money in front of him constituted a request. The dealer should have admitted this incorrect bias to the floor supervisor when he was asked. Given the fact that the floor supervisor was given incorrect information by the dealer, his ruling was fair based on the dealer's incorrect report.

9.47 HEADS-UP BUTTON PLACEMENT AT THE FINAL TABLE

The small blind is always the button when two players are heads up. No one has to be the big blind twice. Depending on where the button is when the third player is eliminated, this may mean that someone skips getting the button or gets the button twice.

9.48 DEAL-MAKING AT THE FINAL TABLE

Players have traditionally been permitted to make deals at the final table in many tournaments, though this practice is forbidden in some tournaments. The logic behind the rule is this: since the prize money comes entirely from player entry fees, it is "their" money, and they have a right to make deals enabling them to chop up the prize money any way they wish to.

There is no official rule about cutting deals at the final table, and some tournaments will not allow it, specifically because they have to have a winner for the sake of TV or because there is a valuable prize to be won such as a bracelet, necklace, and trophy. However, deals are sometimes cut unofficially and the house may help, for example, by bringing out a calculator and figuring a fair split of the remaining prizes based on players' chip stacks and position relative to the button. Sometimes the house institutes a "don't ask, don't tell" policy. This policy allows deals provided they are done away from the table and the house gets to award the prizes exactly as announced, thus leaving it to the players to re-divide the spoils after the tournament is over.

When deals do occur, they must be unanimous among the remaining players and are usually done proportionally to chip count.

Some tournaments won't permit *all* of the prize money to be chopped up among the players but will allow a portion of the money to be set aside and divided by player agreement, as long as a portion of the prize pool remains to be competed for. Competing for the undivided money allows a champion to be determined and for the tournament to be played to its conclusion.

With the advent of televised poker tournaments and the presence of sponsorship money to supplement player-financed prize pools, it is antithetical to the interests of television and sponsors to allow this procedure to continue.

Also antithetical to sponsor and television interests is the common procedure of players trading "pieces" of one another, or having one player backing another player he might wind up competing against during the tournament.

We believe that the appearance of a conflict of interest

can be as detrimental to televised and sponsored poker as a conflict of interest itself, but we still understand the need for players to hedge their risks, especially where player-funded prize pools are concerned.

We recommend that players be forbidden to make deals in any televised or sponsor-funded events (fully or partially sponsor funded), or in any events that come under the auspices of a tour, players' association, or any other tournament-sanctioning body.

We recommend that notwithstanding any tour, tournament, or sponsor-initiated rules to the contrary, any prize-sharing arrangements of more than 5 percent that is made between players be disclosed in writing prior to the beginning of the event. We also recommend that any sponsorship or backing arrangements between players be disclosed in like manner. If a nonplaying person or organization is backing two or more players in the same event, this arrangement should also be disclosed in writing.

With all of this as preface to a compelling issue, we recommend that players be allowed to make deals at the final table as long as the prize money is solely funded by player entry fees, and the tournament's host or sponsoring entity does not declare otherwise.

9.49 CANCELED EVENTS*

Management reserves the right to cancel or alter any event at its sole discretion in the best interest of the casino or its players.

♥ ♠ ♦ ♣

PART FIVE

Rules We'd Like to Change

We're opinionated. We're also experienced poker players who are aware that rules in most poker rooms, just like laws in society, often take a long time catching up with the realities of day-to-day life. There are some rules that are traditional in poker rooms, yet we believe ought to be changed, because better procedures can be put in place when enabled by new rules.

1. BETTING CIRCLES

These are beginning to come into general use but not rapidly enough. We recommend that tables be marked with an elliptical white ring about eight to twelve inches from the rail that follows the contour of the table. Players should be obligated to push their chips beyond the white betting circle when betting, raising, or calling. Any chip movements taking place between the betting circle and the rail will not be construed as action.

We believe this will go a long way to ameliorate disputes as to whether a player's chip movements were *forward action* and therefore a bet or a call, or whether they were simply acts of chip shuffling that have no bearing on a player's decision to act. Furthermore, the use of betting circles makes it easier for the dealer to reach the chips, thus promoting dealers' health and happiness and making the game go faster, too.

2. LETTER-OF-THE-LAW VERSUS SPIRIT-OF-THE-GAME

Many card rooms do not have a stated policy regarding a conflict between a narrowly framed interpretation of the rules and the spirit and traditions of poker. We recommend that whenever a narrowly construed (letter-of-the-law) decision yields an unfair result, or a result not in keeping with the spirit of the law, the best interests of the game, and the traditions of poker, the floor supervisor be encouraged to render a decision yielding a fair result.

Rules should always be interpreted in such a sway that the player holding the best hand is awarded the pot. This is consistent with the best interests of the game, and the traditions of poker.

While this is more a case of *approach* and *attitude* than *rule,* casinos should make their philosophical approach known to customers and employees alike.

3. SHORT BUY-INS

The most common form of the one-short-buy-in-per-session rule occurs when a player goes all-in and loses, then purchases a number of chips that are too few to meet the minimum buy-in threshold for that game. We recommend that whenever a player with less than the minimum buy-in purchases additional chips that still do not provide enough chips to meet the table's minimum buy-in, it should be considered a short buy-in—without regard to whether he went all-in and lost the previous hand.

4. TRIGGERING KILL POTS

In most casinos if the second pot—the one that would trigger a kill—is split due to a tie, the pot is still killed by the player who has now won one pot outright and tied the next one. We recommend this alternate rule: Whenever a leg-up player splits the next pot, it does not trigger a kill. The kill button remains face down with that player, who still has a leg up for the next hand.

INTERPRETATION NOTE

We prefer this rule because imposing the kill on a player who ties the hand can be a detriment to action on the part of players who suspect they may have a tied hand and have to post a full kill after having won a smallish pot.

5. ASKING TO SEE CALLED HANDS

In most casinos any participant in a hand may ask to see a hand that was called. Allowing players to see called hands protects them against collusion, which is the goal of this rule. But this rule is often bent to the point that it is applied solely to get a read on an opponent's playing style, or worse yet, to annoy and irritate him.

We recommend that this rule be done away with, and

the following rule be adopted: any player who has been dealt-in may ask to see any hand that has been called, even if the opponent's hand or the winning hand has been mucked. This rule is intended to detect possible collusion, and the requesting player must be able to substantiate the reason for asking to see a hand.

By requiring that the player asking to see a called hand have a substantial reason to do so, this procedure goes a step further than the traditional rule that allows anyone to see a hand at any time.

6. MUST-MOVE GAMES

To protect an existing game a *must-move* or *forced-move* game may be established and maintained as though it were a waiting list. Players are moved to the main game as seats in the main game become available.

We recommend that players be given a limited option regarding transfers into the main game. If a player prefers to remain in the must-move game, the floor supervisor should ask for volunteers for the main game and select players based on their place on the must-move list.

If no volunteers can be found for the main game, then the floor supervisor will move the player at the top of the must-move list into the main game. If a mandatory move is required and a player refuses to go, he is removed from the must-move game and not permitted to play in a game of that type and limits for two hours.

7. DEAD-BUTTON RULE STANDARDIZATION

Two major variations for blind rules are prevalent: the "forward moving button" and the "dead button." When a dead button is used, a player can be in the dealer position more than once a round, but there'll always be one big and one small blind per hand.

Under forward-moving button procedures, the button always advances, even if someone gets up and leaves in the midst of his or her blinds. When this happens, it is sometimes necessary to have two big blinds and one small blind, or two small blinds and one big blind in the same hand to equalize the blinds with the forward-moving button.

With the increase in interest in tournament poker, coupled with the fact that the dead button is used almost exclusively in tournaments, in the interest of uniformity we recommend standardizing on the dead-button procedure in tournaments and cash games alike.

8. RESPONSIBILITY FOR CHIPS LEFT ON TABLES

Rule 2.36 is "Management is not responsible for cash or chips left on the table by players, whether or not the amount is verified by a floor supervisor or security cameras. Management also bears no responsibility for chips or money left on the table in the case of theft or natural disaster. Nevertheless, a player who wants to keep his seat at the table must leave his chips on the table." We believe that if players are required to keep their chips or money on the table, then management should be responsible for their safekeeping.

9. THE AUTO F-WORD RULE

As much as we dislike profanity, we agree with Jan Fisher that the rule to *automatically* institute a time-out penalty to a player who uses the F-word needs to be modified so that it is not automatic. Floor supervisors should strongly enforce the rule that prevents players from abusing each other, but the F-word rule should be enforced only on a case-by-case basis. For example, we suggest it be overlooked if it is used in the context of a joke and isn't in violation of FCC restrictions or laws.

✳️✳️✳️✳️✳️✳️✳️✳️

This story was submitted by World Poker Tour Announcer, former publisher of *Cardplayer* Magazine, tournament director and WSOP bracelet winner Linda Johnson.

TOPIC
The F-Word Rule: The Case of the Penalized Storyteller

Linda reported that she once heard an interesting tale from a disgruntled player (let's call the player Ruth) at a well-known casino. Ruth explained that one time, right after she won a hand, the losing player muttered, "F . . . g unbelievable." When the dealer didn't react, Ruth called the floor over to ask if there was a penalty for using the F-word. The floor asked Ruth what her question was, and Ruth said that the player had "used the F-word."

The floor asked the dealer if he had heard the word used and the dealer said that he had only heard the player mumble something. The floor then asked

Ruth to repeat exactly what had happened. This time Ruth quoted the offending player and in her quote actually used the real word. The floor explained that the casino had a strict rule against the use of this word and said he would now have to penalize both players for using the offensive word!

After more discussion, the floor did accept Ruth's appeal and let her go with a warning this time, only on the grounds that she was not a regular.

Assessment

We agree with Linda Johnson that this is one of the worst rulings ever.

INDEX